FLYING COLORS

A Guide to Flags from Around the World!

By ROBERT G. FRESSON

CONTENTS

INTRODUCTION 4
GLOSSARY 6

CROSSES AND SALTIRES 8
Greece...10
Switzerland 12
United Kingdom 14
Flags with the Union Jack 16
Georgia 17
TRIBANDS 18
France 20
Flags of Central America 22
Canada 24
Mongolia 26
Colombia 27
Spain 28
Germany 30
DIAGONALS 32
Vanuatu 34
Eritrea 35
PAN-ARAB COLOURS 36
Saudi Arabia 38
Turkey 40
CRESCENT MOONS 42
Libya 44
Afghanistan 45
Brunei 46
Maldives 47
ANIMALS 48
Mexico 50
Kiribati 52
Moldova 53
St Lucia 54

STARS 56
China 58
Israel 60
Nauru 61
Brazil 62
United States of America 64
PAN-AFRICAN COLOURS 66
Swaziland...68
Kenya 69
Zimbabwe..70
Mozambique 71
South Africa 72
Botswana 74
Madagascar.......................................75
BI-COLOURS....................................76
RED AND WHITE 78
Qatar 80
Bahrain 81
Cyprus 82
Kosovo 83
Mauritius 84
Guyana 85
SUNS AND CIRCLES 86
India 88
Macedonia 90
Kyrgyzstan 91
Japan...92
South Korea 94
RED, WHITE AND BLUE 96
Paraguay...98
Thailand 99
Russia 100
Nepal 102

MAPS 104-109

You can use the maps at the back of the book
to find the locations of countries that you
don't already know.

This is a book all about the flags of the world.

You may have seen these flags...

Fluttering from the roof of a palace,

Standing in long lines outside an important government building,

Hanging out of a window,

Waving from the top of a tall ship,

Painted on the face of a football supporter,

Or sticking out of a fine cheese!

In fact, you can find flags all over the place, in every country on the planet, and even on the moon!

But why do flags look the way they do?

Why are there 13 stripes on the flag of the USA?
Why is the French flag blue, white and red?
Why is there a big red circle in the middle of the flag of Japan?

These questions, plus many, many more, will be answered by this book!

WHERE DO FLAGS COME FROM?

The first flags didn't really look like flags. In prehistoric times, powerful people demonstrated their position with tall staffs sporting emblems at the top that showed people who was in charge and what group they belonged to. These symbols of power were called '*VEXILLOIDS*'.

Silk fabric was developed in ancient China. The Chinese used it to make vexilloids with fabric banners, which were more lightweight and easier to see from a distance. Over the centuries, these fabric vexilloids spread across Asia and into the Middle East and Europe.

 In Medieval Europe of the 12th century, banners were flown in battle to identify kings and military leaders.

In the 17th century, flags became standardised and simplified. They were used on ships for identification.

By the 19th century, the modern idea of a flag as a national symbol was established, and by the end of the 20th century all the countries of the world had designed a flag to represent themselves.

THE FLYING COLOURS
GLOSSARY

VEXILLOLOGY = THE STUDY OF FLAGS

Reading this book, you may see some unfamiliar words. They belong to the language of vexillology and are used to describe the features of flags. These are some of the most important terms.

THE PARTS OF A FLAG

UPPER HOIST - The top-most quadrant closest to the flag pole.	**UPPER FLY** - The top-most quadrant furthest from the flag pole.
LOWER HOIST - The bottom-most quadrant closest to the flag pole.	**LOWER FLY** - The bottom-most quadrant furthest from the flag pole.

FIELD

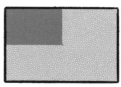

CANTON

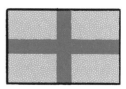

CROSS

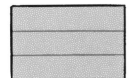
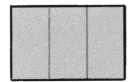

| HORIZONTAL TRIBAND | VERTICAL TRIBAND | PANEL BORDER | LOZENGE |

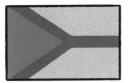
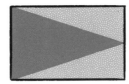

| SALTIRE | TRIANGLE PALL | PILE | DISC |

| BEND | ENHANCED BEND | REDUCED BEND | FIMBRIATED BEND |

FIMBRIATION - Where an element of a flag is bordered in another colour

INTRODUCING

THE

VEXILLOLOGISTS

Let our crack team of colourful experts guide you through the flags of the world!

| BLUE | YELLOW | BLACK | GREEN | RED | WHITE |

You will see them on many pages, demonstrating how flags are put together.

All over the world, the shape of a cross symbolises the Christian faith. However, up until the 4th century, the primary symbol for Christianity was actually a fish! In 326 AD St Helena is said to have found the cross on which Christ was crucified. This popularised the idea of a cross representing martyrdom and salvation.

-

A saltire is an X-shaped cross. Some examples of saltires have been found on Roman coins from the 4th century.

-

Many countries feature crosses in their flags, as Christianity is an important part of their national identity.

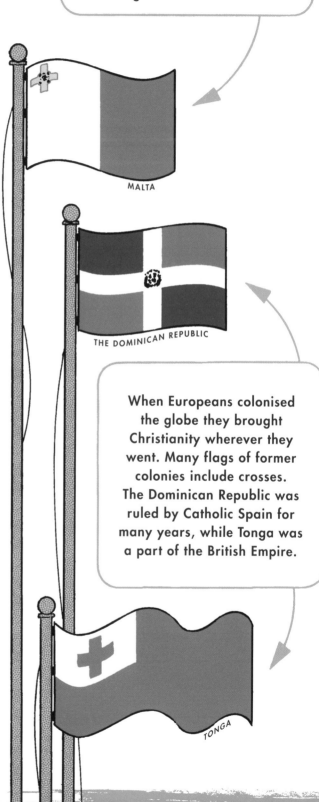

The George cross in the Maltese flag represents a military medal given to Malta in 1942 by King George VI of Great Britain.

MALTA

THE DOMINICAN REPUBLIC

When Europeans colonised the globe they brought Christianity wherever they went. Many flags of former colonies include crosses. The Dominican Republic was ruled by Catholic Spain for many years, while Tonga was a part of the British Empire.

TONGA

ICELAND

NORWAY

FINLAND

SWEDEN

DENMARK

Both Burundi and Jamaica became independent nations in the 1960s. Burundi is the only country in Africa to use a saltire. Jamaica's saltire merges the shapes of the Scottish flag with the colours of the African National Congress.

BURUNDI

JAMAICA

The flag of Denmark is the oldest national flag in the world, dating back to the 12th century. Over the years, the off-centre cross became popular with Denmark's neighbours, becoming known as the Nordic Cross.

THE FLAG OF GREECE

A.K.A THE 'BLUE & WHITE'

A white
equilateral cross

- in -

a blue
square canton

- on -

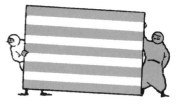

a striped field of
blue and white

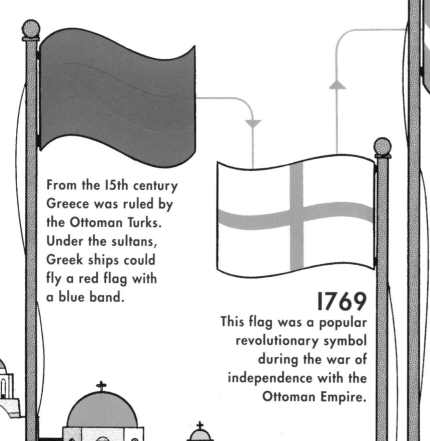

From the 15th century Greece was ruled by the Ottoman Turks. Under the sultans, Greek ships could fly a red flag with a blue band.

1769

This flag was a popular revolutionary symbol during the war of independence with the Ottoman Empire.

1822

When the war was won, this became the new national flag of Greece, with the striped flag used on ships as a naval ensign.

The cross is symbolic of the Greek Orthodox faith.

1978

The striped naval ensign proved very popular and was frequently flown alongside the national flag of the white cross on the blue field. Eventually it became the official flag of Greece.

The nine stripes represent the nine syllables in the phrase **Ελευθερία ή Θάνατος** (Eleftheria i Thanatos) which translates as "Freedom or Death". This was the Greek battle cry against the Ottoman Empire during the revolution.

The exact shade of blue has never been fixed. It can be anywhere between a pale sky blue and a deep royal blue.

THE FLAG OF
SWITZERLAND

A white equilateral cross — on — a square red field

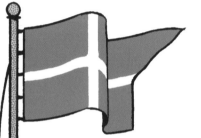

1000

The Holy Roman Empire used a white cross on a red field to symbolise the purity of the emperor and the blood of Christian martyrs.

1600s

The *flammé* design was one of many square military flags that were used in the confederation of Swiss states.

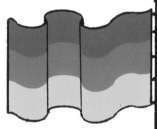

1798

The French invaded the Swiss confederacy and declared this as their new flag. It only lasted two years.

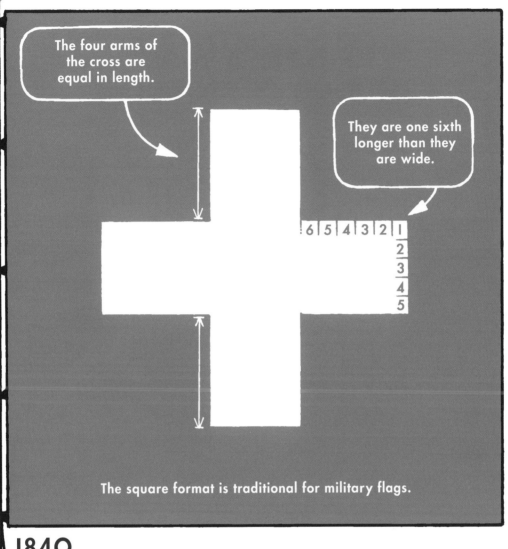

The four arms of the cross are equal in length.

They are one sixth longer than they are wide.

6 5 4 3 2 1
2
3
4
5

The square format is traditional for military flags.

1840

Swiss generals reverted to the white cross on a red background.

The Swiss flag is one of only two square flags in the world.
Can you find the other one?

THE FLAG OF THE UNITED KINGDOM

A.K.A THE 'UNION JACK'

- with -
- on -
- on -

A red cross with a white border

a red saltire

a white saltire

a dark blue field

The flag of England is called the St George's Cross and it dates back to the days of the crusades.

Patron saint of Scotland, St Andrew, was crucified on an X-shaped cross. The flag of Scotland is called the St Andrew's Saltire.

In 1606, King James I united England and Scotland and combined the two flags under the 'Union Flag'.

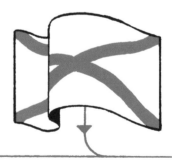

The St Patrick's Saltire is an old flag of Ireland. In 1801, Ireland became part of the United Kingdom and the red saltire was added to the design.

LOOK CLOSELY!

The design of the **UNION JACK** is not symmetrical.

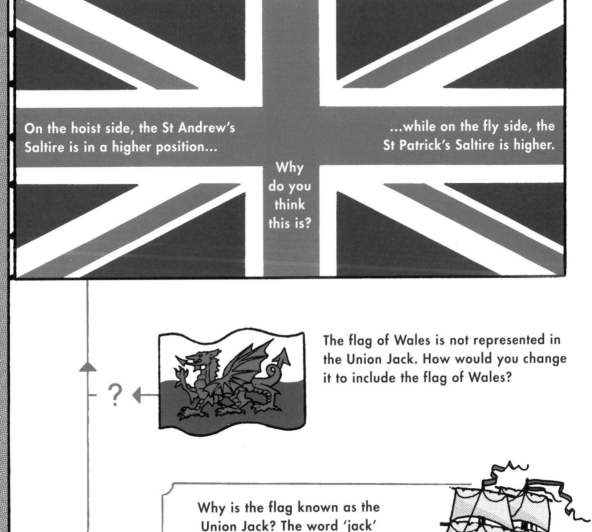

On the hoist side, the St Andrew's Saltire is in a higher position...

...while on the fly side, the St Patrick's Saltire is higher.

Why do you think this is?

?

The flag of Wales is not represented in the Union Jack. How would you change it to include the flag of Wales?

Why is the flag known as the Union Jack? The word 'jack' might come from the 'jackstaff' of a ship, or it might have been a nickname for James I.

FLAGS
WITH THE
UNION JACK

At its height, the British Empire ruled over 24% of the world. You can see the legacy of the empire in the flags of some of its former colonies...

FIJI
This flag places the Union Jack on a light blue field and features the national coat of arms. An attempt to remove the colonial elements of the flag was abandoned in 2016.

AUSTRALIA
The Union Jack has been in the canton of Australia's flag since 1901. The flag also features the seven-point Commonwealth Star and the Southern Cross, a distinctive constellation visible in the southern hemisphere.

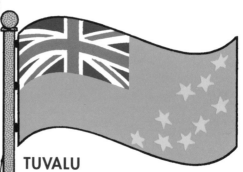

TUVALU
The nine stars on the Tuvalu flag symbolise its nine islands. The Union Jack was removed in 1996, but put back a year later because the new version of the flag was so unpopular.

NEW ZEALAND
Although it is often confused with the flag of Australia, in 2016 people voted to keep this flag instead of opting for a new design.

As well as these countries there are 28 other territories, states and provinces that use the Union Jack.

THE FLAG OF
GEORGIA

A red
cross

- with -

a red Bolnisi cross in
each quarter

- on -

a white
field

1918

The flag of the Republic of
Georgia was dark red with
a horizontal bi-colour canton
in black and white.

1921

The Soviet Union
invaded Georgia and
applied their own
designs to the flag.

1991

After the Soviet
Union dissolved, the
republican flag was
brought back into use.

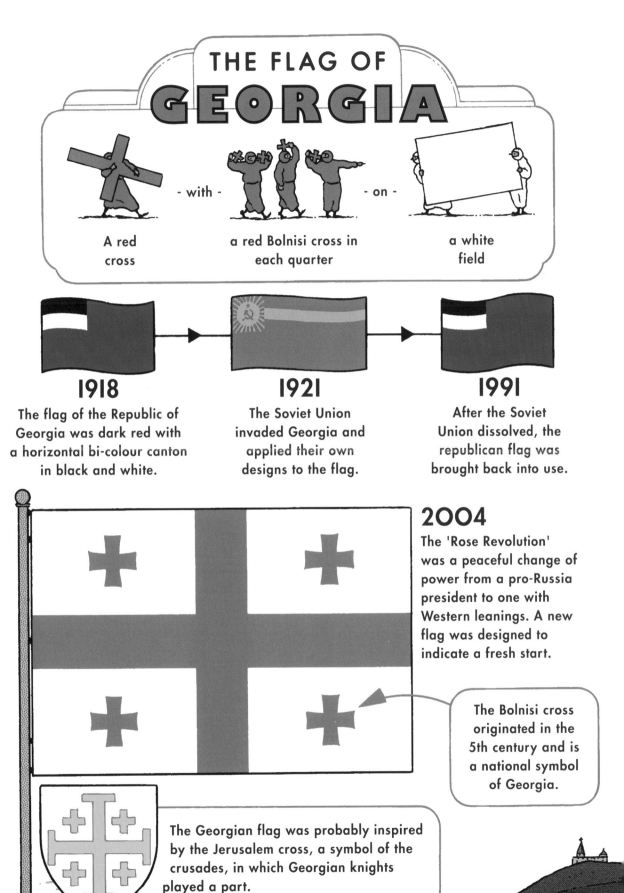

2004

The 'Rose Revolution'
was a peaceful change of
power from a pro-Russia
president to one with
Western leanings. A new
flag was designed to
indicate a fresh start.

The Bolnisi cross
originated in the
5th century and is
a national symbol
of Georgia.

The Georgian flag was probably inspired
by the Jerusalem cross, a symbol of the
crusades, in which Georgian knights
played a part.

TRIBANDS

Over 40% of the world's flags use a triband in their design. Even the planet Mars has one!

MARS

Most tribands can be traced back to old European flags. The flag of Austria is said to date back to the 1100s. Legend has it that Duke Leopold V was inspired when he took the belt from his blood-soaked coat and revealed a perfectly white strip where the belt had been.

-

During the colonial era, European countries introduced tribands to the countries they occupied. Upon independence, many former colonies continued to use tribands.

Many of these vertical tribands are influenced in their design by the French Tricolour, which came to represent republicanism and liberty from the old aristocratic regimes.

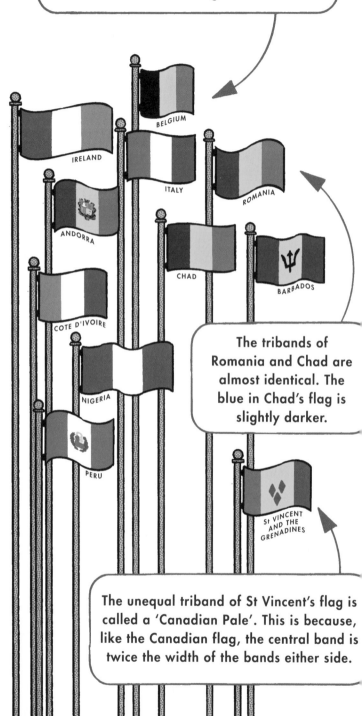

The tribands of Romania and Chad are almost identical. The blue in Chad's flag is slightly darker.

The unequal triband of St Vincent's flag is called a 'Canadian Pale'. This is because, like the Canadian flag, the central band is twice the width of the bands either side.

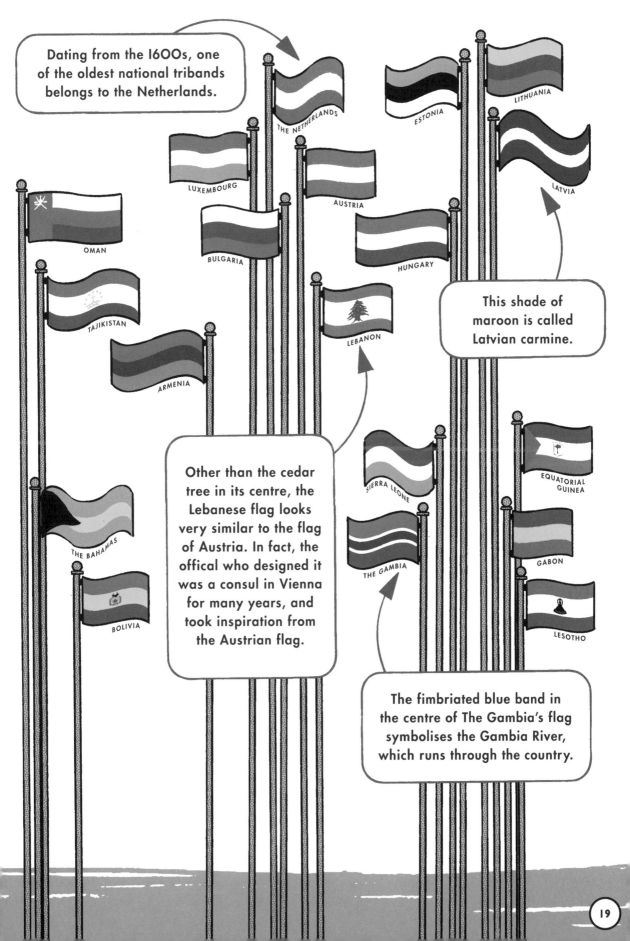

Dating from the 1600s, one of the oldest national tribands belongs to the Netherlands.

THE NETHERLANDS

ESTONIA

LITHUANIA

LATVIA

LUXEMBOURG

AUSTRIA

OMAN

BULGARIA

HUNGARY

This shade of maroon is called Latvian carmine.

TAJIKISTAN

LEBANON

ARMENIA

Other than the cedar tree in its centre, the Lebanese flag looks very similar to the flag of Austria. In fact, the offical who designed it was a consul in Vienna for many years, and took inspiration from the Austrian flag.

SIERRA LEONE

EQUATORIAL GUINEA

THE BAHAMAS

THE GAMBIA

GABON

BOLIVIA

LESOTHO

The fimbriated blue band in the centre of The Gambia's flag symbolises the Gambia River, which runs through the country.

THE FLAG OF
FRANCE

A.K.A 'LE TRICOLOUR'

A vertical triband of

blue   white   - and -   red.

In the 15th century, the white battle standard of Joan of Arc featured small golden lilies, known as *fleurs de lis*. White and gold came to symbolise French royalty.

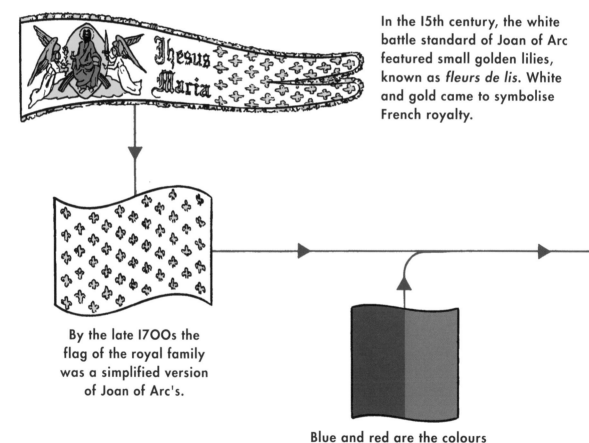

By the late 1700s the flag of the royal family was a simplified version of Joan of Arc's.

Blue and red are the colours of Paris. They have been used in the city's coat of arms since 1358.

Blue is the colour of St Martin. He allegedly sliced off half of his blue cloak to give to a beggar who was freezing in the snow.

White was added to 'nationalise' the otherwise Parisian colours. It refers to France's history of monarchy.

Red is the colour of St Denis, patron saint of Paris.

In another interpretation, the colours relate to France's motto:

LIBERTÉ --------- ÉGALITÉ --------- FRATERNITÉ

The Tricolour was introduced in 1794 but went in and out of use until 1830, when the citizen-king Louis Philippe brought it back for good.

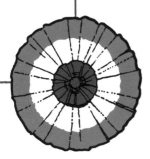

After the storming of the Bastille in 1789, the Marquis de Lafayette declared that revolutionaries should wear a red, white and blue rosette on their hats (called a cockade).

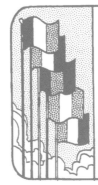

The Tricolour has had a great influence on flag design worldwide. From the mid-1800s, many newly independent countries chose to use a vertical triband to symbolise their republican national identity.

CENTRAL AMERICAN FLAGS

During the 1820s and 1830s several countries in Central America gained independence from Spain and formed the

'FEDERAL REPUBLIC OF CENTRAL AMERICA'

The triband flag reflected the government's republican ideals.

The colours represented Central America's geographical position between the Pacific and Atlantic Oceans.

1823

In 1839, civil war caused the Federal Republic to dissolve and the nations separated. However, they all took elements of the republican flag with them.

GUATEMALA

Guatemala shifted to a vertical triband like neighbouring Mexico.

EL SALVADOR

The Salvadorian coat of arms replaced the original crest and the blue bands were made darker.

HONDURAS

The five blue stars in the centre represent the five former states of the republic.

NICARAGUA

The flag of Nicaragua is the closest to the original republican flag.

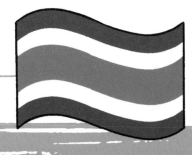

COSTA RICA

The flag of Costa Rica was significantly redesigned in 1848. It was influenced by the French flag and the blue was darkened to match it.

THE FLAG OF
CANADA

A red maple leaf

on an
- unequal -
triband of

red, white and red

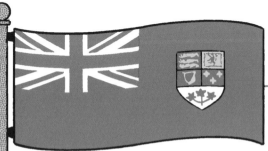

For most of its colonial history, Canada flew the flags of Britain and France. Until the 1960s, the flag was a British Red Ensign with a shield from the Canadian coat of arms on the fly.

THE GREAT FLAG DEBATE

In 1963, Prime Minister Lester B Pearson formed a committee to choose an official flag for Canada. The Red Ensign was popular amongst English Canada, but a problem for French Quebec, who objected to the Union Jack.

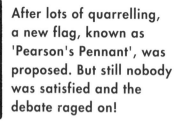

After lots of quarrelling, a new flag, known as 'Pearson's Pennant', was proposed. But still nobody was satisfied and the debate raged on!

The white area is double the width of the red.

1964
Canadian parliament decided on this flag, designed by George Stanley.

The maple leaf has been a popular Canadian national symbol since the 19th century.

But what do the 11 points on the maple leaf stand for? Nothing at all! They just look good when the flag is blowing in the wind.

THE FLAG OF
MONGOLIA

on the
- hoist -
side of

The national symbol
in yellow

a triband of red, blue
and red

Blue represents
the sky.

Red represents
the resilience of
the Mongolian
people in
the face of
hardship.

The national symbol
of Mongolia is called
the *Soyombo*.

1992

Fire represents revival, growth and
the family hearth.

The sun and moon indicate the importance of
nature in Mongolian culture.

The downward pointing triangles represent
arrowheads and the death of enemies.

The two slim, flat rectangles stand for honesty and
justice between rulers and their people.

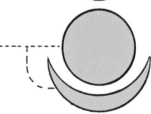

The yin-yang symbol represents man
and woman in harmony.

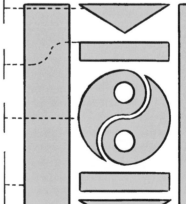

THE FLAG OF
COLOMBIA

- then -

- under -

A blue band

a red band

a double-width yellow band

Yellow represents gold.

Blue represents the sea, rivers and sky.

Red represents the battle for independence and the resilience of the Colombian people.

1861

This flag was designed by the revolutionary freedom fighter, Francisco de Miranda. He thought that the primary colours of yellow, blue and red were very powerful. He wrote that his destiny was "to create in [my] land, a place where primary colours are not distorted."

VENEZUELA

From 1821 to 1831, Colombia was part of a larger country called Gran Colombia which also included Ecuador and Venezuela. Can you see the shared history of these countries in their present day flags?

GRAN COLOMBIA

ECUADOR

THE FLAG OF
SPAIN

The Spanish coat of arms	hoist centre of - two red bands - on -	a yellow field

1785
King Charles III chose this flag because it looked distinctive at sea.

1931
The monarchy was overthrown and purple was added to the republican flag.

1938
The new dictator, Francisco Franco, changed the flag back to red and yellow but added a black eagle.

1981
Franco's changes were eliminated from the coat of arms. This is how the Spanish flag looks today.

The yellow band is twice the height of the red bands. Any triband flag with these proportions is called a 'Spanish Fess'.

The coat of arms is made up of the arms of the four Medieval kingdoms of Spain: Castile, Leon, Aragon and Navarre. The pomegranate at the base represents Granada. The pillars either side represent Gibraltar and Cueta. The motto, *plus ultra*, means 'further beyond', referring to Spain's colonial strength.

Catalunya, a fiercely independent region of Spain, has long campaigned to separate from the rest of the country. Many people fly the Blue 'Estalada' from their windows to show support for this goal.

THE FLAG OF
GERMANY

A _horizontal triband_ of

black

red

- and -

gold

1866-1918

This black, white and red triband was adopted when Prussia united with 21 other German states to create a confederation. It eventually became the German Imperial Flag.

1919

The Weimar Republic adopted the flag we know today. The colours are thought to originate from the uniforms of anti-Napoleon student rebels of the 1820s.

1933

When Adolf Hitler came to power he introduced the flag of the Nazi Party. It used the imperial colours and featured a swastika, an ancient Indian symbol that the Nazis used to represent Aryan superiority.

1948

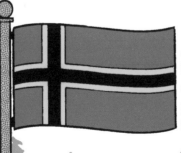

After World War II, Germany was split in two; the communist East and the capitalist West. Proposals for flags were put forward, like this one that features the Weimar colours in a Nordic Cross.

Both East and West Germany eventually chose to return to the Weimar Republic triband. However, in 1959, East Germany decided to add their coat of arms to the flag.

West Germany was very angry and called this the 'divider flag'.

1989

After the fall of the Berlin Wall in 1989, many East Germans cut the coat of arms out of their flags, and the triband was reinstated.

DIAGONALS

One word best fits the visual effect of a diagonal: *dynamic!*

Graphic designers use diagonal lines or text to create a sense of momentum and progress. It is for this very reason that diagonal patterns can be found in these nations' flags.

Without exception all of these countries are former colonies of European powers. They use diagonals to reflect their aspirations for the future. A diagonal band, or *bend* as it is known in vexillology, helps to distinguish these designs from the rectangular tribands and crosses of European flags.

ST KITTS AND NEVIS

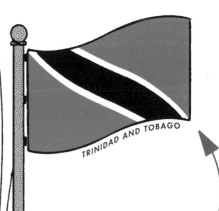

TRINIDAD AND TOBAGO

The fimbriated black bend of Trinidad and Tobago's flag is 'descending', in that it goes from the upper hoist to the lower fly. This is less common in vexillology but typical in heraldry, where it is called a *bend dexter*, meaning 'right' in Latin. An ascending bend is called a *bend sinister* meaning 'left'.

REPUBLIC OF THE CONGO

DEMOCRATIC REPUBLIC
OF THE CONGO

TANZANIA

NAMIBIA

SEYCHELLES

THE MARSHALL ISLANDS

SOLOMON ISLANDS

The flag of the Republic of the Congo has an 'enhanced bend', as it goes from the top edge to the bottom, rather than corner to corner. The Democratic Republic of the Congo has a 'reduced bend', reaching between the hoist and fly edges only.

The flags of the Seychelles and the Marshall Islands feature bends that widen towards the fly. In both cases this is meant to symbolise a dynamic young country moving towards a prosperous future.

THE FLAG OF
VANUATU

The national emblem   - in -   a black triangle   - enclosed by -   a yellow pall with black fimbriations   - dividing -   a field of red and green.

When the Pacific archipelago of Vanuatu gained independence from France and the United Kingdom in 1980, they chose to design a flag using red, green and black; colours popular amongst Melanesian countries.

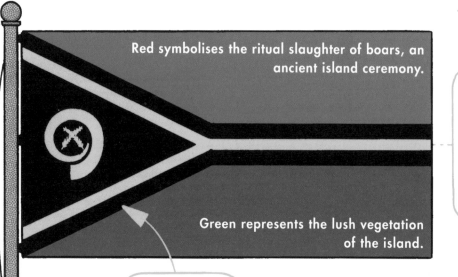

Red symbolises the ritual slaughter of boars, an ancient island ceremony.

Green represents the lush vegetation of the island.

The yellow pall symbolises both the shape of the Vanuatu islands and the light of the gospel.

Black is for the people of Vanuatu.

A spiral boar's tusk, symbolising prosperity, is often worn on a pendant by islanders. Inside are leaves of a local fern called *namele*.

THE FLAG OF
ERITREA

 - in -  - dividing -

| The national emblem | a red pile | a field of green and blue |

1952

After a period of British colonial rule, the United Nations helped Eritrea become autonomous. The blue field and olive wreath were influenced by the flag of the UN.

1961

Eritrea was annexed to Ethiopia. The Eritrean People's Liberation Front (EPLF) fought a bloody battle against this new occupation. The star in their flag demonstrates the group's socialist revolutionary ideals.

1993

When the country finally became independent, the EPLF's star was replaced with the previous flag's wreath to represent peace.

PAN-ARAB COLOURS

The Pan-Arab colours are white, black, green and red.

Throughout the centuries, various Arab dynasties ruled over parts of North Africa and the Middle East. The flags of these dynasties were one single colour, the most famous being the Umayyads, the **Abassids**, the Fatimids and the Hashemites. In 1916, a group of Arab nationalists led a revolt against the ruling Ottoman Turks. They flew a flag featuring all the colours of the four dynasties. The flag of this Arab Revolt went on to inspire the flags of many Arab countries.

-

In 1952, republican revolutionaries in Egypt overthrew the king and ended the British occupation of Egypt. They flew a triband of red, white and black and this combination became known as the Arab Liberation flag. Arab states wishing to align themselves with the ideals of republicanism chose to base their flags around this triband.

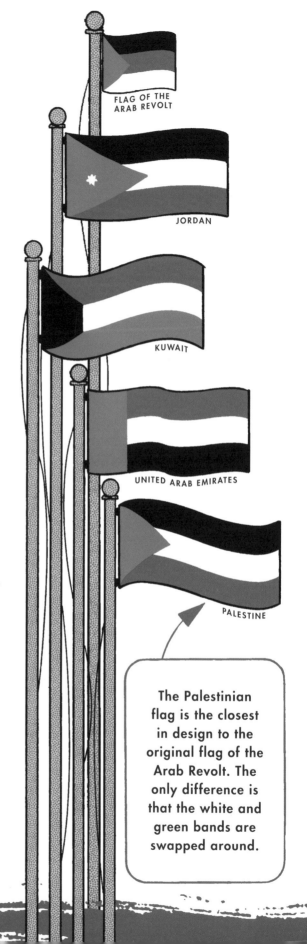

FLAG OF THE ARAB REVOLT

JORDAN

KUWAIT

UNITED ARAB EMIRATES

PALESTINE

The Palestinian flag is the closest in design to the original flag of the Arab Revolt. The only difference is that the white and green bands are swapped around.

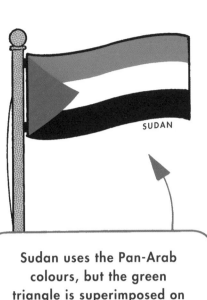

SUDAN

Sudan uses the Pan-Arab colours, but the green triangle is superimposed on the Arab Liberation triband. This reflects Sudan's close relationship with Egypt.

The emblem in the centre of the Egyptian flag is called the 'Eagle of Saladin'. It is based on a carving of an eagle on the wall of the Cairo Citadel and came to represent Arab identity during the 1950s.

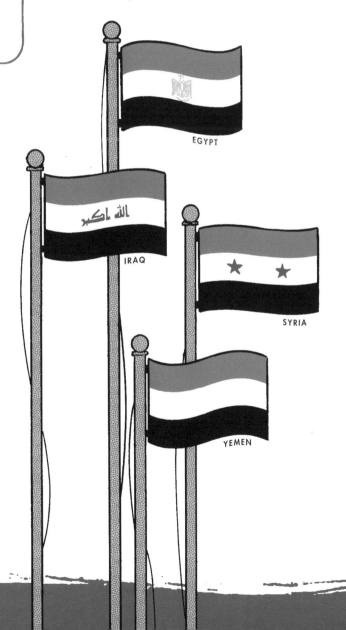

EGYPT

IRAQ

SYRIA

YEMEN

THE FLAG OF
SAUDI ARABIA

The *Shahada* in white

- above -

a white sabre

- on -

a green field

The Saudi flag has remained largely unchanged since the early 20th century.

The colour green is linked to Fatima, the Prophet Muhammed's daughter.

Representational art is forbidden in Islam, so the art of calligraphy was highly developed.

The inscription is the *Shahada*, an Islamic declaration of faith, which translates as:

"There is no god but God: Muhammad is the messenger of God".

It is the same orientation on both sides of the flag, so it can always be read correctly.

The sabre points towards the hoist side, in the direction that you read the Shahada; right to left.

The design of the flag was influenced by the ultra-religious Wahhabi sect, which has been using the Shahada on its flags since the 18th century. The sabre was added in 1902 to represent the militancy of Saudi faith.

? Although other national flags have small inscriptions, the Saudi flag is the only one that features writing as its central design.

THE FLAG OF
TURKEY

A.K.A 'AL BAYRAK' (THE RED FLAG)

A white moon
and star

- on -

a red
field

The crescent and star symbol has roots reaching deep into Turkey's ancient history. It has been found in Sumerian excavations from the 13th century BC, representing the pagan moon and sun gods. Later, the symbol appeared in 1st century Byzantium, representing the Roman moon goddesses, Luna and Diana.

1844

The Islamic Ottoman Empire was at the centre of the Eastern and Western worlds for over six centuries. The star and crescent was introduced as a state symbol in the late 18th century, and became the empire's flag.

1936

The flag has remained relatively unchanged since the rule of the Ottomans. The crescent became slimmer and the number of points on the star changed from five to eight and back to five.

CRESCENT MOONS

It is common to think of the crescent moon and star as an Islamic symbol, but in fact it predates Islam by about 2,000 years, appearing in ancient Mesopotamian artwork from around 1500 BC.

Only when the symbol was appropriated by the Ottomans did the star and crescent become associated with Islam. The Ottoman Empire lasted over 600 years and at its height its influence stretched from Central Europe to East Asia and down to North Africa.

Over the course of the 20th century, many Muslim countries took inspiration from the power of the Ottomans, incorporating the moon and star into their designs, and cementing its association with the Islamic faith.

At one time or another Algeria, Tunisia and Azerbaijan were all controlled by the Ottoman Empire.

AZERBAIJAN

TUNISIA

ALGERIA

MAURITANIA

The Mauritanian flag is one of only two world flags that does not use red, white or blue. Can you find the other?

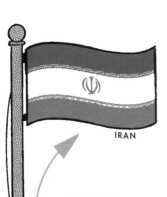

IRAN

TURKMENISTAN

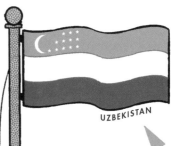

UZBEKISTAN

Iran uses crescents in an unusual way. The four crescents are arranged to make the shape of a tulip, a Persian symbol of martyrdom.

Turkmenistan boasts the world's most complex flag, with a pattern that represents the nation's carpet-making industry.

The flag of Uzbekistan has 12 stars alongside its crescent. They represent the signs of the zodiac.

COMOROS

PAKISTAN

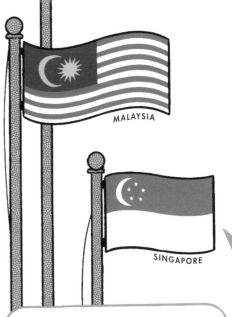

MALAYSIA

SINGAPORE

Originally the Malaysian flag had a five-pointed star. However, this was seen to be too suggestive of communism so more points were added.

Singapore is the only non-Muslim nation to include a crescent its flag. The five stars are influenced by the flag of China.

THE FLAG OF
LIBYA

A white moon
and star

on an
- unequal -
triband of

red, black
and green

1951

Libya gained independence
and was ruled by King Idris Al
Senussi. His emblem of a white
crescent moon and star on a
black background was inspired
by the Turkish flag.

1969

The monarchy was
overthrown by Colonel
Qaddafi. He took a flag
inspired by the Arab
Liberation Flag.

1977

Angry with Egypt, Qaddafi
changed the flag to a plain
green field. It represented
Qaddafi's aim to find new
water sources and create an
agricultural 'green revolution'.
At the time it was the only
national flag in the world
made up of a single colour.

2011

Qaddafi was overthrown and the
1951 flag was reinstated.

THE FLAG OF AFGHANISTAN

The national emblem

on a
- vertical -
triband of

black, red and green

The nation of Afghanistan has gone through many political upheavals over the past century, and this is reflected in the fact that its flag changed 21 times – more than any other flag in the world!

1901

A new emblem was devised for Afghanistan. It shows a mosque facing Mecca surrounded by flags, cannons, swords and sheaves of wheat.

1928

Once independent from British rule, King Amanullah Kahn made the flag a triband. He was probably influenced by the flag of Germany.

2013

After countless changes in power – kings, communists and Taliban – the 1901 emblem and Amanullah's colours can still be found on the present day flag.

THE FLAG OF
BRUNEI

The national
emblem

- on -

a black and white
reduced bend

- on -

a yellow
field

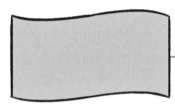

Up until the 20th century, Brunei's
flag was a plain yellow field,
representing the Sultan.

In 1906, when Brunei became a
British protectorate, two diagonal
bands were added to the flag,
representing Brunei's chief ministers.

When the country
adopted a
constitution in
1959, the national
emblem was added
to the flag.

The emblem of Brunei was designed in the
15th century. It consists of a crescent bounded by the
benevolent hands of government and topped by a
parasol, representing monarchy. The Arabic inscriptions
read: "Always render service under the guidance of
God" and "Brunei, abode of peace".

THE FLAG OF
THE MALDIVES

  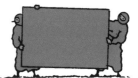

A white crescent moon   - on -   a green panel   - on -   a red field

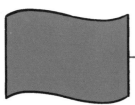

For many years, the Maldivian flag was a plain red field; the same as Oman, Qatar, Kuwait and other Middle Eastern territories.

1926

It became necessary to have a more specific national flag. The green panel and white cresent referenced Islam.

1965

The Maldives gained independence and altered the flag. The hoist stripes were removed and the crescent flipped to face the fly side.

ANIMALS

Both mythical and real-life creatures feature on flags. Animals often symbolise traits that we would like to see in ourselves, like bravery, strength or beauty. But even countries with no animals in their flags have a national animal. Do you know the national animal of your country?

MONTENEGRO

ALBANIA

DOMINICA

GUATEMALA

THE SISSEROU PARROT OF DOMINICA

The colouring of this parrot makes Dominica one of a few countries to use purple in its flag.

THE RESPLENDANT QUETZAL OF GUATEMALA

The green Quetzal represents freedom from Spanish rule for the people of Guatemala.

THE DOUBLE-HEADED EAGLE OF ALBANIA AND MONTENEGRO

The double-headed eagle is an ancient symbol dating back to the Romans and Byzantines. It was popularised in the Balkans during the 15th century when Albanians revolted against the Ottomans.

THE GREY CROWNED CRANE OF UGANDA

The crane is actually a military symbol in Uganda, left over from British rule.

THE KUMUL OF PAPUA NEW GUINEA

Papua New Guinea's native bird of paradise represents the unification of the country.

THE GOLDEN LION OF SRI LANKA

With its *Kastane* sword, the golden lion stands for the bravery of the Sri Lankan people.

DRUK THE THUNDER DRAGON OF BHUTAN

Bhutan is actually named after this mythical dragon, which holds four jewels in its claws.

THE FLAG OF MEXICO

 The national emblem · on a vertical triband of ·  green, white and red

1810

The standard of the Virgin Guadalupe is considered by some to be the first flag of Mexico. It was carried by a Catholic priest, Miguel Hidalgo, when he led the first uprising against Spanish rule.

This was the flag of the army that finally defeated the Spanish. This army was called the 'Three Guarantees', because it promised to protect the country's religion, unity and independence.

1821

When independence was finally achieved, a flag similar to the one we know today was adopted. However, the eagle was wearing a crown and had no serpent in its talons.

1968

Over time, the central emblem changed to what we see today.

The national emblem depicts an ancient Aztec legend, in which the founder of Tenochtitlan (now Mexico City) saw an eagle with a snake in its beak perched atop a cactus in the middle of a lake, and founded the city on the spot where the vision appeared. Underneath is a wreath of oak and laurel tied in a ribbon of the national colours.

You would be forgiven for thinking that the flag of Mexico is based on that of Italy. In fact, the Mexican flag has been in use for longer and uses a darker green. However, both were influenced by the republican French Tricolour.

THE FLAG OF
KIRIBATI

 - with -  - on -

A yellow rising sun and frigate bird | three white wavy bands | a field of red and blue

1937

Kiribati was part of the Gilbert and Ellice Islands, a colony of the British Empire.

The coat of arms depicts a native golden frigate bird flying over a rising sun.

The 17 sun rays represent the 16 Gilbert Islands and Banaba Island.

1979

Kiribati became an independent nation. The new flag was based on the colonial coat of arms.

Three white stripes represent three groups of islands; Gilbert, Phoenix and Line.

THE FLAG OF
MOLDOVA

The national coat of arms

on a
- vertical -
triband of

blue, yellow and red

The Principality of Moldavia (1346–1859) had a red flag with the head of an aurochs, an extinct European ox, surrounded by a rose, a crescent and a star.

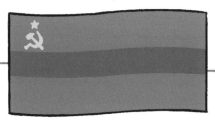

The country was shunted from Ottoman rule to the Soviet Union to Germany, Romania and back to the Soviet Union. In 1952, it adopted the Soviet banner with a green stripe through it to represent agriculture.

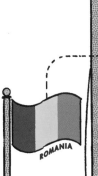

ROMANIA

The blue is lighter than in the Romanian flag.

The aurochs symbol is framed by an eagle.

1990

With the breakdown of the Soviet Union, a blue-yellow-red Romanian triband was adopted to demonstrate Moldovan solidarity with its neighbour. Recently, alternative flags have been proposed to make the flag more distinctively Moldovan.

THE FLAG OF
ST LUCIA

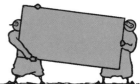

A yellow triangle — on — a black triangle with white fimbriations — on — a light blue field

1939

Since the 16th century, St Lucia was fought over by the British and French. Finally, in 1814, the British took control and St Lucia flew a colonial ensign.

The St Lucia crest featured a cross formed of two sticks of bamboo. The quadrants contain two fleurs de lis, representing France, and two Tudor roses, representing England.

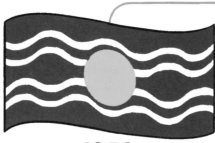

1958

St Lucia became a part of the West Indies Federation along with other Caribbean island nations that had been British colonies. The flag represented the sun shining on the Caribbean Sea. This union proved unsuccessful and it dissolved in 1962.

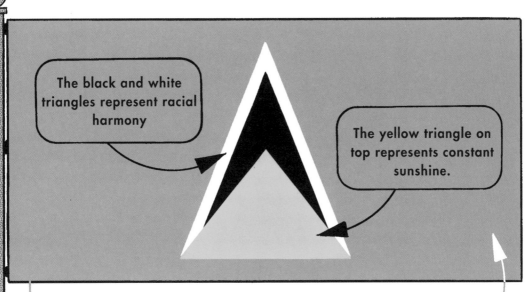

1967

St Lucia became an Associated State of Britain, whereupon a new flag was created. Full independence was granted in 1979 and the Union Jack was lowered for the last time.

The blue field represents the Atlantic Ocean and the Caribbean Sea, which surround the island.

The overlapping triangles also represent the Pitons, two striking volcanic cones that rise up from the sea and serve as a national symbol for St Lucia.

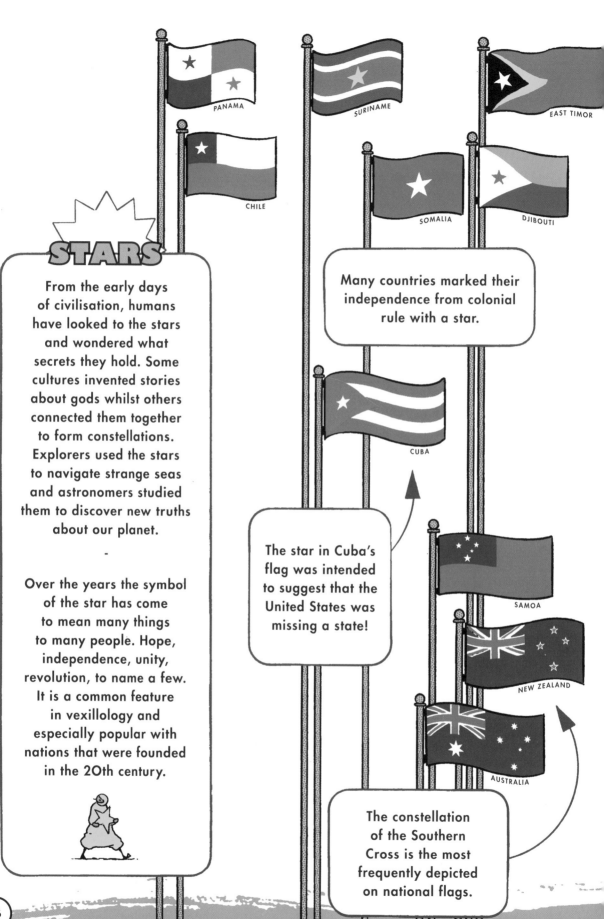

PANAMA

SURINAME

EAST TIMOR

CHILE

SOMALIA

DJIBOUTI

STARS

From the early days of civilisation, humans have looked to the stars and wondered what secrets they hold. Some cultures invented stories about gods whilst others connected them together to form constellations. Explorers used the stars to navigate strange seas and astronomers studied them to discover new truths about our planet.

-

Over the years the symbol of the star has come to mean many things to many people. Hope, independence, unity, revolution, to name a few. It is a common feature in vexillology and especially popular with nations that were founded in the 20th century.

Many countries marked their independence from colonial rule with a star.

CUBA

The star in Cuba's flag was intended to suggest that the United States was missing a state!

SAMOA

NEW ZEALAND

AUSTRALIA

The constellation of the Southern Cross is the most frequently depicted on national flags.

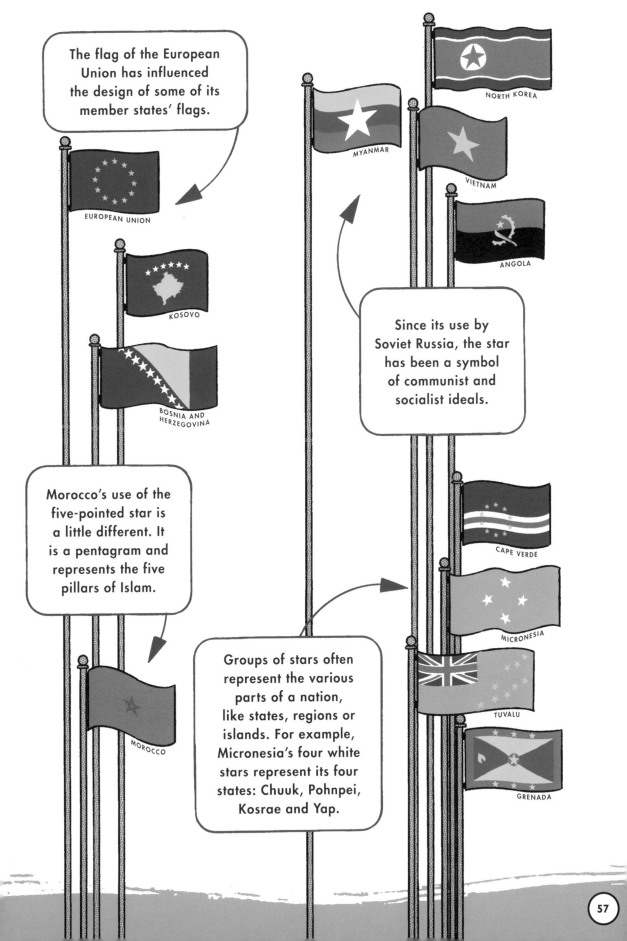

The flag of the European Union has influenced the design of some of its member states' flags.

EUROPEAN UNION

KOSOVO

BOSNIA AND HERZEGOVINA

Morocco's use of the five-pointed star is a little different. It is a pentagram and represents the five pillars of Islam.

MOROCCO

MYANMAR

Groups of stars often represent the various parts of a nation, like states, regions or islands. For example, Micronesia's four white stars represent its four states: Chuuk, Pohnpei, Kosrae and Yap.

NORTH KOREA

VIETNAM

ANGOLA

Since its use by Soviet Russia, the star has been a symbol of communist and socialist ideals.

CAPE VERDE

MICRONESIA

TUVALU

GRENADA

THE FLAG OF CHINA

Five gold stars | in the - canton of - | a red field

1889

China was ruled by emperors for over 2,000 years. Yellow was the colour most associated with the Emperors of China. The Qing dynasty had a yellow flag depicting the 'Azure Dragon', a symbol of power and strength, with the 'flaming pearl' of good fortune.

1912

After the overthrow of the Qing dynasty, the Five-Coloured flag was adopted. Each colour represents an ethnic group in China (from top to bottom): Han, Manchu, Mongol, Hui and Tibetan.

1928

The official flag of the Republic of China was known as 'White Sun, Blue Sky and a Wholly Red Earth'. After the communist revolution, this flag was banned by Mao Zedong. It is still flown in Taiwan.

1949

The flag of the People's Republic of China was adopted after a national competition to design a new flag. The winning entry was designed by Zen Liansong.

The red field symbolises the communist revolution and is also the colour of fortune and joy in Chinese culture.

The big star represents the communist party and there is a small star for each of the four social classes: workers, peasants, urban bourgeoisie and national bourgeoisie. Notice how they all point to the big star.

Five is an important number in Chinese culture.

Yellow represents the bright future of communism.

A blue hexagram

- between -

two horizontal blue bands

- on -

 a white field

The flag of Israel was designed in 1891, over 50 years before the country physically existed. It was made for the newly formed Zionist movement, which aimed to create a Jewish homeland. When the state of Israel was established in 1948, the design became the official national flag.

The blue and white stripes were inspired by the design of the *tallit*, the Jewish prayer shawl, which is white with blue stripes along the bottom.

The hexagram is not an exclusively Jewish symbol, although it has been used in Jewish culture since the 16th century. In the 19th century, Jewish communities in Eastern Europe began to use it as an easily identifiable 'logo' that could rival the crucifix. It became known as the 'Star of David'.

THE FLAG OF
NAURU

A white
12-pointed star

- beneath -

a thin
gold band

- on -

a dark
blue field

The flag of the Pacific island of Nauru represents its geographical position; one degree south of the Equator and to the west of the International Date Line. Nauru became independent in 1968, after many years of German, British, Japanese and Australian control.

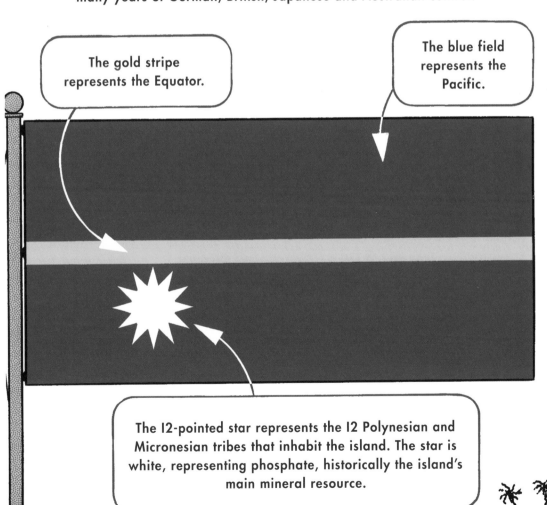

The gold stripe represents the Equator.

The blue field represents the Pacific.

The 12-pointed star represents the 12 Polynesian and Micronesian tribes that inhabit the island. The star is white, representing phosphate, historically the island's main mineral resource.

THE FLAG OF
BRAZIL
A.K.A THE 'AURIVERDE'

The national motto - and - 27 white stars - on - a blue disc - in - a yellow lozenge - on - a green field

1822

Brazil declared independence from the Portuguese Empire, and Pedro I became the ruler of the Empire of Brazil. Green was the colour of Pedro's family crest, whilst yellow was that of his wife's, Empress Maria Leopoldina of Austria. The coat of arms featured an armillary sphere (an ancient navigational device that can also be found in the flag of Portugal). The white stars around it represent the provinces of Brazil.

1889

The Empire was overthrown and the Republic of the United States of Brazil was formed. For five days this provisional flag was flown, but it was ultimately determined to be too similar to the flag of another United States....

1889

The flag of Brazil is known as the *Auriverde* – meaning the gold and green.

The motto means 'Order and Progress' and comes from the words of French philosopher, August Comte "Love as a principle and order as the basis; progress as the goal".

The flag takes inspiration from some elements of the 1822 flag, however, its modern design reflects the aspirations of the new republic.

The central emblem, known as the 'celestial sphere', depicts, as viewed from above, the constellations over Rio de Janeiro on November 15, 1889, the night the republic was established.

The 27 stars represent the 26 states of Brazil, plus its capital, Brasilia.

THE FLAG OF THE
USA

A.K.A *'THE STARS and STRIPES'*

 - on - - in the canton of -

Fifty
white stars

a blue
rectangle

a field of 13 red and
white stripes

The 50 white stars are known as the 'union'
and represent the 50 states that make up the
United States of America.

Although there is no official
significance to the colours, it
has been said that white is
for purity, red for hardiness
and valour and blue for
perseverance and justice.

The 13 horizontal red and white stripes
represent the 13 British colonies that
declared independence in 1776.

64

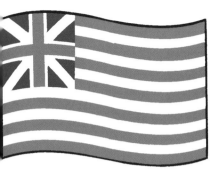

1776

For the first year of its independence, the United States had a flag with the pre-1801 Union Flag in the canton. It is thought that this flag was influenced by that of the British East India Company.

1777

Legend has it that an upholsterer called Betsey Ross designed the first 'Stars and Stripes' flag based on a drawing by George Washington. However, it was actually designed by one of the signatories of the declaration of independence, Francis Hopkinson.

The American flag has been through 28 variations since its conception. Every time a state was added, another star joined the canton. The number of stripes stayed the same. Up until 1912, the position of the stars in the canton was not regulated, leading to some flamboyant arrangements....

1818

1837

1859

1861

1865

PAN-AFRICAN COLOURS

There are two sets of Pan-African colours. They have different origins but both have come to represent the liberation and heritage of the African peoples.

-

The first set is green, gold and red. These were the colours of the Empire of Ethiopia, which was the only African country to successfully resist colonial occupation in the late 1800s. When other African countries won their independence, many drew inspiration from the strength of Ethiopia and used a combination of the three colours in their new flags.

-

The second set is red, black and green. In 1917, the leader of the Pan-African movement, Marcus Garvey, created a triband of red for the noble blood of Africans, black for the people and green for the rich land of Africa. His aim was to enable self-reliance and nationhood in black people around the world, and his message inspired the design of many African flags.

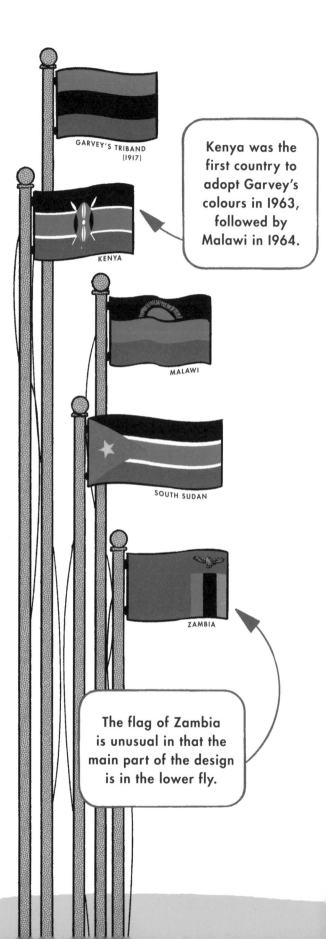

GARVEY'S TRIBAND
(1917)

KENYA

MALAWI

SOUTH SUDAN

ZAMBIA

Kenya was the first country to adopt Garvey's colours in 1963, followed by Malawi in 1964.

The flag of Zambia is unusual in that the main part of the design is in the lower fly.

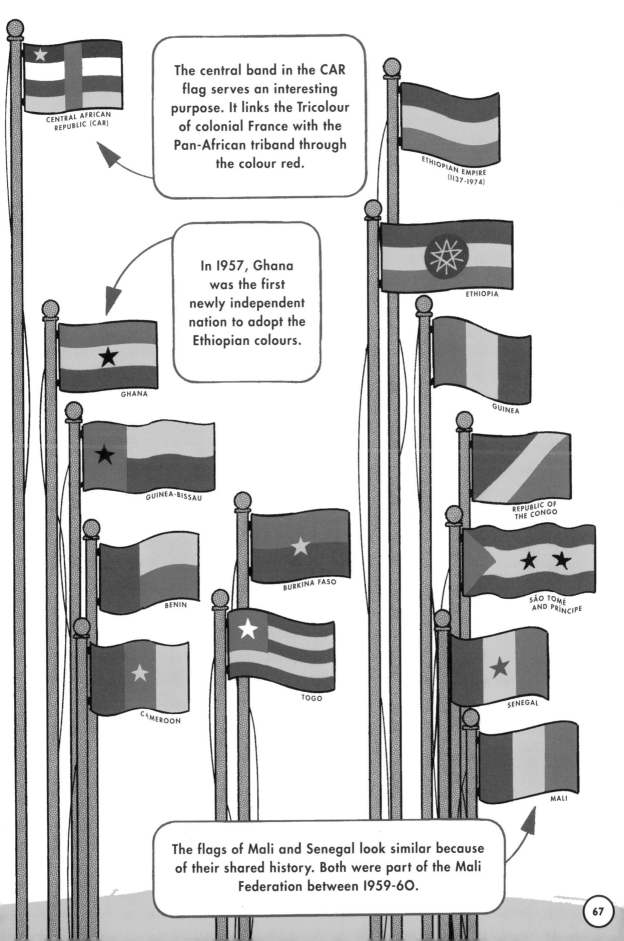

CENTRAL AFRICAN
REPUBLIC (CAR)

The central band in the CAR
flag serves an interesting
purpose. It links the Tricolour
of colonial France with the
Pan-African triband through
the colour red.

ETHIOPIAN EMPIRE
(1137-1974)

In 1957, Ghana
was the first
newly independent
nation to adopt the
Ethiopian colours.

ETHIOPIA

GHANA

GUINEA

GUINEA-BISSAU

REPUBLIC OF
THE CONGO

BENIN

BURKINA FASO

SÃO TOMÉ
AND PRÍNCIPE

CAMEROON

TOGO

SENEGAL

MALI

The flags of Mali and Senegal look similar because
of their shared history. Both were part of the Mali
Federation between 1959-60.

THE FLAG OF
SWAZILAND

| A black and white Nguni shield | - on - | two yellow spears and a staff | - decorated with - | three blue *injobo* | - on - | a red band with yellow fimbriations | - on - | a field of blue |

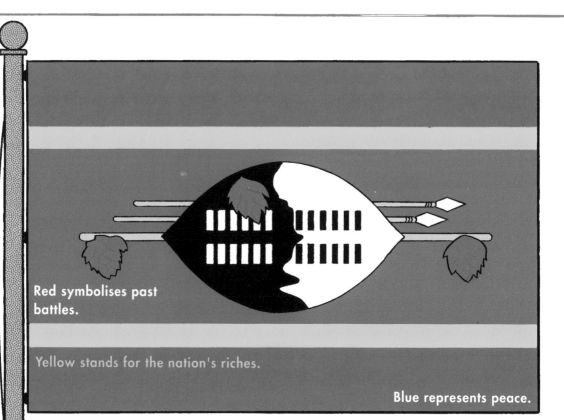

Red symbolises past battles.

Yellow stands for the nation's riches.

Blue represents peace.

1968

When Swaziland won its independence from British colonial rule, it chose a flag that represented the cultural heritage and traditions of its people. A traditional ox-skin shield, used by the Nguni people is accompanied by by two *tikhali* (spears) and an *umgobo* (staff). These are all decorated by blue *injobo* – ceremonal feather decorations symbolising royalty. The shield pattern is meant to represent peace between races.

THE FLAG OF
KENYA

- on -

- on -

A black, red and white
Maasai shield

a red band with
white fimbriations

a field of black
and green

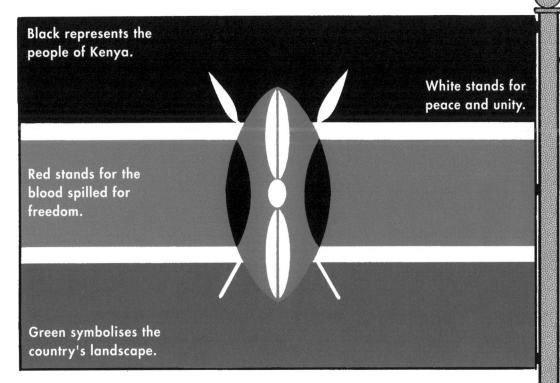

Black represents the
people of Kenya.

White stands for
peace and unity.

Red stands for the
blood spilled for
freedom.

Green symbolises the
country's landscape.

1963

Like Swaziland, Kenya was a British colony, known as British East
Africa. After a long and bloody fight for independence, the nation
finally won its freedom from imperial rule. The new flag was
based on the Garvey triband and featured a Maasai warrior shield
on two crossed spears, representing the defence of the nation's
independence and values.

THE FLAG OF
ZIMBABWE

A yellow Zimbabwe Bird

- on -

a red star

- on -

a white triangle with black fimbriations

- at the hoist of -

seven stripes of green, yellow, red and black

1923
Zimbabwe was named Southern Rhodesia after British businessman, Cecil Rhodes, whose company controlled the area.

1968
A white minority government declared independence. Their new flag featured a depiction of the 'Zimbabwe Bird', an ancient soapstone statue found at the ruins of the city of Great Zimbabwe.

1979
Guerilla fighters overthrew the white government and instated a temporary flag in the Pan-African colours.

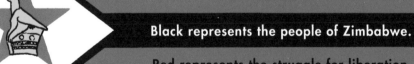

The white triangle represents peace and progress.

The red star represents socialism.

Black represents the people of Zimbabwe.

Red represents the struggle for liberation.

Yellow represents mineral wealth.

Green represents fertile land.

1980
Zimbabwe was finally granted full independence and a new flag was designed with the Zimbabwe Bird in pride of place.

THE FLAG OF
MOZAMBIQUE

The national emblem

- on -

a yellow star

- in -

a red triangle

- on -

a green, black and yellow triband with white fimbriations

The white fimbriations represent peace.

Green represents fertile land.

Black represents the people of Mozambique.

Red represents the struggle for independence.

Yellow represents mineral wealth.

Mozambique became fully independent from Portugal in 1975. The flag features a hoe and an AK-47 crossed over an open book. The book symbolises education while the hoe stands for agriculture and the gun for defence of the land. In 1983, the symbol was updated to include a yellow Marxist star. The flag of Mozambique is the only flag other than Guatemala to include a firearm in its design.

THE FLAG OF
SOUTH AFRICA

A black triangle with yellow fimbriations	a green pall with white fimbriations	a field of red and blue
- in -	- on -	

1910

Despite gaining nominal independence, South Africa still flew a British colonial flag. This was not very popular with the Afrikaner descendants of Dutch colonialists.

1928

The white minority government adopted a new flag that represented unity between the British and the Afrikaner populations. It was based on a historical Dutch flag called the Prince's Flag – an orange, white and blue triband.

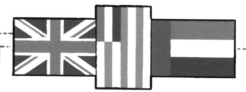

The three small flags represented the provinces of South Africa. The Union flag stands for the previously British-run Natal and Cape Colony. The middle is the Boer republic of Orange Free State and the right is the South African Republic.

1994

When the era of apartheid (racial segregation) finally ended,
Nelson Mandela's party, the African National Congress (ANC),
came to power and introduced a new flag. Although this flag
was only intended to be temporary, it captured a spirit of
optimism and unity and was made permanent in 1996.

Can you see how the South African flag cleverly
combines the colours of the ANC flag with those
of the nation's former colonists, Britain and the
Netherlands? The 'Y' shape of the design is said
to represent a converging of paths – a
merging of past and present. Very few
flags use six colours in their designs.

BOTSWANA

A black band with
white fimbriations

- on -

a field of
light blue

Light blue represents the sky, but also water
– a scarce resource in a dry country.

1966

When Botswana gained
independence from British rule,
a flag was chosen that was
deliberately different from that
of apartheid-era South Africa,
emphasising the peaceful coexistence
of races in Botswana.

The black and white stripes
represent harmony between people
of African and European descent.
They also symbolise the stripes
of the zebra, Botswana's
national animal.

THE FLAG OF
MADAGASCAR

A white rectangle — on the hoist side of — a field of red and green

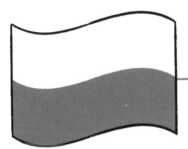

Red and white were the colours of the Merina people, whose proud kingdom governed central Madagascar until their defeat and occupation by the French. The colours probably originated from the Indonesian ancestors of the Merina.

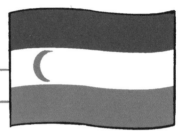

1885
Madagascar became a protectorate of France, and flew a flag based on the Tricolour.

1958
When Madagascar was freed from French rule, green was added to the Merina's colours of red and white. The decision to arrange the colours in this unusual formation indicates a desire to distance the country from French colonial influence.

BI-COLOURS

Bi-colours are flags split either horizontally or vertically between two colours. They are closely linked with the history of heraldry in Europe.

In Europe during the Middle Ages, if you were a member of a noble family, you had a coat of arms. This was an identifying symbol that told people how important you were. Many of these families were so powerful that they ruled over nations, and so, over time, the coat of arms came to symbolise nationality.

When these countries wanted to design a flag, some of them reduced their coat of arms down to its basic colours. Some European bi-colour flags have their origin in this process of simplification. Can you see the similarities between these flags and the coats of arms that influenced them?

VATICAN CITY

A gold key over a silver key translates to yellow and white.

LIBERTAS

SAN MARINO

Three silver towers on a blue sky are simplified to white and blue.

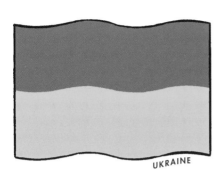

UKRAINE

The colours of the Ukrainian flag can be traced to the coat of arms of the Medieval principality of Galicia.

PORTUGAL

For most of its history, the flag of Portugal was a bi-colour of blue and white, corresponding to the blue and white shield on the coat of arms.

But in 1911, a new government introduced green and red as the colours of Portuguese republicanism.

LIECHTENSTEIN

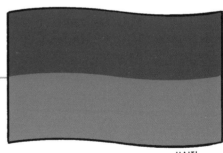

HAITI

When Liechtenstein turned up to the 1936 Olympic Games in Berlin, the delegation discovered they had exactly the same flag as Haiti, so the following year they added a yellow crown to the canton of their flag.

The origin of the Haitian bi-colour is a bit different. When Haiti won independence from colonial France it is said the new leader ripped out the white centre of the French Tricolour and had the remaining colours stitched back together.

RED AND WHITE

Some flags are confusingly similar.
Poland, Monaco and Indonesia all utilise a horizontal bi-colour in red and white. However, the similarities are accidental, and the origins of each one are quite distinct.

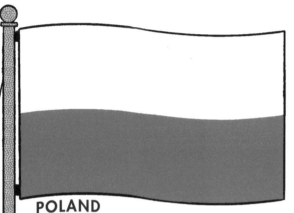

POLAND

The flag of Poland is derived from its Medieval coat of arms, a white eagle on a red shield.

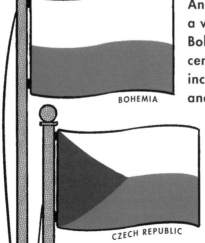

BOHEMIA

CZECH REPUBLIC

Another Medieval kingdom with a white over red bi-colour was Bohemia. By the early 20th century it had expanded to include the lands of Moravia and Slovakia and become Czechoslovakia. In 1920, a blue triangle was added to reflect the ethnic differences in the population. The Czech Republic kept this flag after its separation from Slovakia.

MONACO

Monaco was controlled by the Grimaldi family for hundreds of years. The flag is based on the family's coat of arms, which features a red and white lozenge pattern.

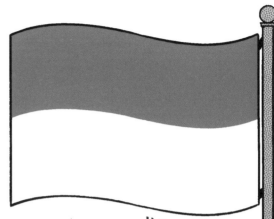

INDONESIA

The flag of Indonesia is different to that of Monaco only in its dimensions. The colours red and white have deep roots in ancient Austronesian mythology – red represented Mother Earth, and white represented Father Sky. Under Dutch colonial rule, this flag was banned. On the eve of a great battle, Indonesian revolutionaries tore the lower blue band from the Dutch flag to create a makeshift Indonesian flag.

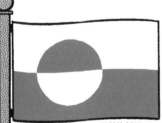

GREENLAND

SINGAPORE

Despite its similarities to the flag of Poland, Greenland is actually a territory of Denmark and borrows its colours from the Danish cross.

Singapore and Indonesia are neighbouring countries with similar flags, but Singapore's flag has different origins. The flag was originally red but this was felt to be too communist, and so the white was added.

THE FLAG OF
QATAR

A white band with a
nine-pointed serrated edge

- on the
hoist
side of -

a field of
maroon

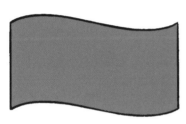

For many decades Qatar and the other
countries on the coast of the Arabian
peninsula flew the plain red flags of the
Kharjite sect of Islam, which controlled that
part of the Persian Gulf.

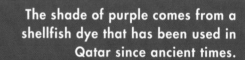

The shade of purple comes from a
shellfish dye that has been used in
Qatar since ancient times.

The nine 'serrations' represent
Qatar's position as the ninth
member of the Emirate states.

1916

The area was fraught with war and
piracy for many centuries, until the
British enforced the General Treaty
of Peace. Part of the agreement was
that the flags should have a white
border.

? Qatar's flag is the
only national flag that
is more than twice as
wide as it is high.

THE FLAG OF
BAHRAIN

A white band with a
five-pointed serrated edge

- on the
hoist
side of -

a field of
red

The five serrations represent the
five pillars of Islam.

Like Qatar, Bahrain flew a plain red
flag until the British decree to add
white. The flag originally had 28
white points. In 1972 it was reduced
to eight and then to five in 2002.

THE FLAG OF
CYPRUS

 - above -  - on -

A map of Cyprus in copper

two green olive branches

a field of white

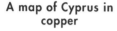 For many decades, Cyprus has been at the heart of an ownership dispute between Christian Greece and Islamic Turkey.

1960

Cyprus became independent and a competition was held to design a new flag. The rules of the competition said the flag should not include blue (the colour of Greece) or red (the colour of Turkey), and should not use the shape of a cross or a crescent. The winning entry was designed by a school-teacher, Ismet Guney.

The copper outline represents the country's rich copper deposits, while the olive branches symbolise peace between Greek and Turkish Cypriots.

 In 1974, Turkey invaded Cyprus and established a self-proclaimed country, The Turkish Republic of Northern Cyprus, with its own flag.

Under a plan for a resolution to the conflict in Cyprus, a new flag was proposed including the blue of Greece and the red of Turkey. However, the plan was shelved and so was the flag.

THE FLAG OF
KOSOVO

 - above -  - on -

Six white stars · a gold map of Kosovo · a blue field

Kosovo is a disputed land between Serbia and Albania. From 1998 to 1999, Kosovan separatists fought a bloody war with Yugoslav troops.

Eventually, in 1999, the UN stepped in and presided over the region.

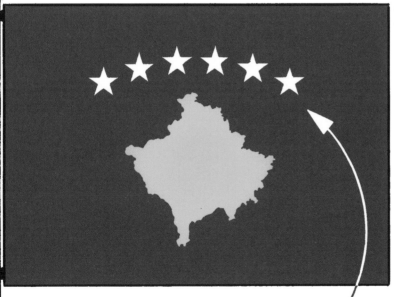

2008

When a competition was held to design a new flag, it was decided to avoid using the black and red of Albania or the Serbian red, white and blue. The double-headed eagle that features on both the Serbian and Albanian flags was also avoided.

The six stars represent the six ethnic groups of Kosovo and also reference the flag of the European Union.

THE FLAG OF
MAURITIUS

A.K.A *'LES QUATRE BANDES'*

Four equal
horizontal
bands of

red

blue

yellow

and green

1923

During its time as a British colony, Mauritius flew an ensign with the Mauritian coat of arms, featuring a stag and a dodo. The now extinct dodo was native to the island.

Red represents the stuggle for independence.

Blue symbolises the Indian Ocean.

Yellow is for the 'light of freedom shining over the island'.

Green is for the lush, subtropical landscape.

1968

When Mauritius gained its independence, it adopted its current flag. It is the only national flag made up of four horizontal stripes.

THE FLAG OF
GUYANA

A.K.A *'THE GOLDEN ARROW'*

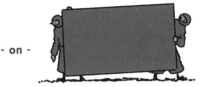

A red triangle with black fimbriations

- on -

a yellow pile with white fimbriations

- on -

a field of green

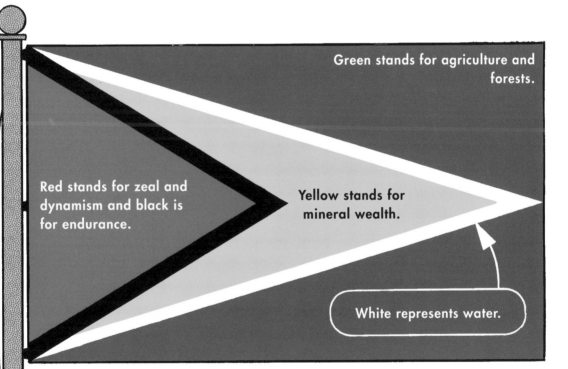

Green stands for agriculture and forests.

Red stands for zeal and dynamism and black is for endurance.

Yellow stands for mineral wealth.

White represents water.

1966

Guyana (formerly British Guyana) adopted this flag upon independence. It was designed by Whitney Smith, an American vexillologist. Smith's original design (pictured right) had a different colour arrangement and no fimbriations. The English College-of-Arms suggested the changes before the flag was officially adopted.

SUNS AND CIRCLES

When you think of the sun, what comes to mind? Heat? Light? Power? Without the sun, life as we know it could not exist. It is an important symbol all across the world, standing for hope, unity, progress or wealth.

-

Flags with sun symbols often belong to countries with an important story of gaining independence and sovereignty. For them, the sun represents the dawning of a new era.

BANGLADESH

NIGER

RWANDA

TAIWAN

THE PHILIPPINES

ANTIGUA AND BARBUDA

NAMIBIA

A circle can be the sun, but it can also be a peaceful, unifying full moon like in the flags of Palau and Laos.

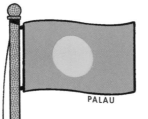

PALAU

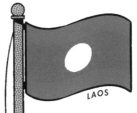

LAOS

The flag of Belize uses a white disc to enclose the national coat of arms, which depicts the country's historically important logging industry.

BELIZE

ARGENTINA

URUGUAY

The flags of Argentina and Uruguay show the 'Sol de Mayo' (Sun of May), a symbol of independence from Spanish rule.

A steppe eagle flies under the Kazakh sun.

KAZAKHSTAN

THE FLAG OF
INDIA

A blue wheel — on a horizontal triband of — orange   white   and green

1863–1947

India had been under British control since the mid-1700s. By the 1860s it was known as the 'British Raj' and ruled over by Queen Victoria as 'Empress of India'.

1921

The leader of the All-India Congress, Mohamdas Karachand Gandhi, chose a flag that would represent his ambition for a free, independent India. The three colours represented the ethnicities of India: Hindu (red), Muslim (green) and others (white). The spinning wheel symbolised Gandhi's aspiration for the country to become self-reliant by manufacturing clothing.

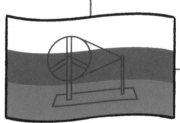

1923

The white became the middle stripe to provide a clear background for the spinning wheel. Gandhi wished to move away from the religious symbolism of the first flag, and the red was changed to a saffron colour. Saffron was said to stand for courage and sacrifice, white for peace and green for faith.

1947

When India finally became independent, the flag changed again. Orange now symbolises disinterest in material gains. White stands for the path of truth, and green for relation to the land.

The flag of India must only be made of a hand-spun cotton or silk cloth called *khadi*. Flying a flag made of other material can be punishable with three years imprisonment!

The spinning wheel was replaced by the 'Ashoka Chakra', a Buddhist symbol of the circle of life and of dharma (cosmic law). It has origins in the 3rd century, when it was used by the Emperor Ashoka, who attempted to unite all of India under one government.

It represents dharma, national unity, progress and motion, and also references Gandhi's spinning wheel.

THE FLAG OF
MACEDONIA

- on -

A yellow sun with
eight rays

a field of
red

1946

When Macedonia became part
of the Republic of Yugoslavia,
it flew a simple red flag with a
five-pointed gold star
in the canton.

1992

A newly independent
Macedonia swapped the
five-pointed star for a
larger, centred
'Vergina Sun'.

THE VERGINA SUN

was the symbol of
Alexander the Great, and his
father, Phillip II of Macedon.
It was first found in 1977 on
the funeral casket of Phillip
II at an archaeological
dig in Greece.

The Greeks were much
angered by Macedonia's use
of the Vergina Sun motif,
which they regarded as
part of their own heritage.
They imposed an economic
blockade on Macedonia and
barred them from flying the
flag at the United Nations.

1995

To placate Greece and ease diplomatic relations,
Macedonia agreed to change their flag. The new
design was still based on the Vergina Sun but
different enough to keep the peace!

THE FLAG OF
KYRGYZSTAN

Two crossing sets of three   - on -   a yellow   - on -   a field of
curved red lines   sun   red

1992

When Kyrgyzstan became independent from Soviet Russia, it was decided to continue using a red flag. However, the red does not relate to communism; it tells another story...

Red actually references a flag carried by a Kyrgyz folk hero, Manas the Noble. The central yellow emblem depicts a view of the roof of a yurt, the tent dwelling of Kyrgyz nomads. Behind this symbol is a sun with 40 rays, symbolising the 40 tribes united under Manas. Together these symbols represent the traditions and history of the Kyrgyz people, as well as solidarity and security.

THE FLAG OF
JAPAN

A.K.A *'HINOMARU'*

 - on -

A red disc   a white field

The official name of the flag of Japan is *Nisshoki*, meaning sun-mark-flag, but most people call it *Hinomaru*, meaning circle-of-sun. It has been in use for well over 1,000 years. The first documented use of the flag was in 1184, but there are stories of the same flag being used centuries earlier. It was officially adopted as the flag of Imperial Japan in 1870.

The red disc stands for the sun.

The white field represents purity.

The Emperor is said to have descended from the sun goddess, Amaterasu, and the sun has always been central to Japanese religion and mythology.

To some, the flag of Japan is a symbol of aggression, particularly in countries such as China and South Korea, which suffered under the hands of Japanese occupation in the early 20th century. A version of the flag, known as the Rising Sun flag, was flown by the Japanese Imperial Navy, and is considered particularly offensive.

Despite the controversy around it, the Rising Sun flag is still considered a symbol of good fortune within Japan and it can be seen on commercial products, advertisements and on the flag of the Japan Maritime Self-Defense Force.

THE FLAG OF
SOUTH KOREA

A.K.A THE 'TAEGUKGI'

 - surrounded by -  - on -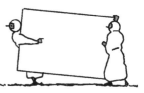

A red and blue *taeguk*

four black trigrams

a white field

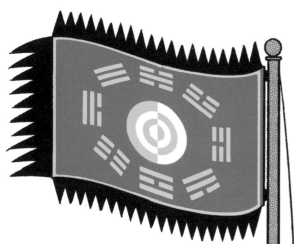

For five centuries, Korea was ruled by the Joseon dynasty. Although they had no official national flag, the Joseon flew this standard. The symbols represented Korean Daoism, and their origins stretched far back to ancient Confucian symbols used for fortune-telling.

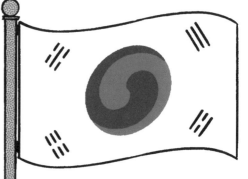

1883

Due to international pressure and modern ideas of nationhood, it was decided that Korea should have a national flag. An inital proposal took influence from the flag of the Chinese Qing dynasty but in the end they went for something more distinctively Korean.

Since it was adopted, the Korean flag has had some minor alterations, but stayed roughly the same.

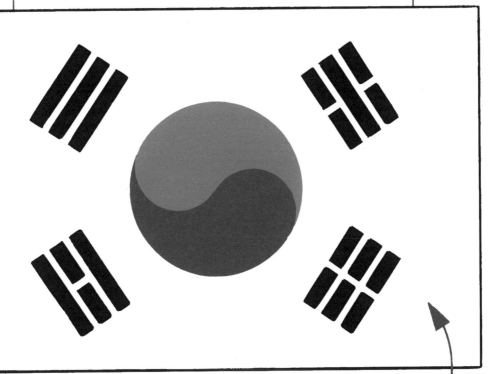

White represents purity. It is also the colour of traditional Korean costume.

The central yin-yang symbol is called the *taeguk*, representing the balance of the universe – negative and positive, good and evil, male and female.

Surrounding the taeguk are four sets of black bars in patterns of broken and unbroken strokes. They are called *kwae*, or trigrams, and each one represents the classical elements of Confucian principles:

| HEAVEN | MOON | SUN | EARTH |
| JUSTICE | WISDOM | FRUITION | VITALITY |

RED, WHITE AND BLUE

The most common combination of flag colours is red, white and blue. See if you can find all the flags in the book with this trio of colours.

PARAGUAY

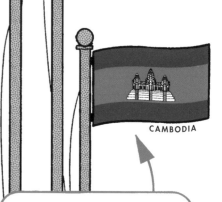
LUXEMBOURG

Although it is very similar to the Dutch flag, the triband of Luxembourg is actually based on the national coat of arms, which features a red lion on a field of blue and white stripes. The blue is lighter than that of the Netherlands.

CAMBODIA

LIBERIA

Cambodia's flag shows the famous temple Angkor Wat in the centre.

From 1822, Liberia was colonised by freed African-American and Carribbean slaves. You can see the influence of the United States in the design of the Liberian flag.

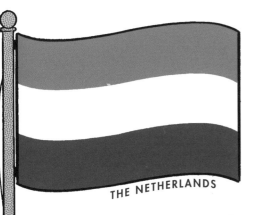

THE NETHERLANDS

THE PAN-SLAV COLOURS

The origin of the Dutch flag goes back to the 16th century, when William I, Prince of Orange, flew a banner of orange, white and blue. Over the years, the orange changed to red. This was the flag that Tsar Peter the Great of Russia saw in 1697, when he visited Europe to learn about shipbuilding. Upon his return to Russia he introduced the Russian triband of white, blue and red, influenced by the flags on Dutch ships.

In 1848, the Pan-Slav Conference in Prague announced white, blue and red as the Pan-Slav colours. The legacy has been carried on in the flags of the Slavic nations of Southern and Eastern Europe.

RUSSIA

SLOVAKIA

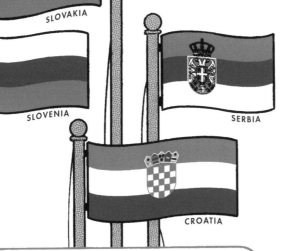

SLOVENIA

SERBIA

CROATIA

BULGARIA

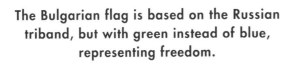

The Bulgarian flag is based on the Russian triband, but with green instead of blue, representing freedom.

THE FLAG OF
PARAGUAY

The national coat of arms - and - the seal of the treasury - on a horizontal triband of - red, white and blue

The flag of Paraguay was adopted during the rule of dictator Jose Gaspar Rodriguez de Francia (1814–40). As an admirer of Napoleon, Francia chose a flag inspired by the colours of the French flag.

Francia's design is unique for having the two sides of the flag differ from one another.

On the obverse side is the national emblem: a yellow star surrounded by an olive branch, representing peace, and a palm branch, representing honour.

The reverse of the flag depicts the seal of the treasury. In it a lion guards a red phyrgian cap mounted on a staff. The phyrgian cap was worn by freed Roman slaves and French revolutionaries and represents liberty. 'Paz y Justicia' means peace and justice.

THE FLAG OF
THAILAND

A blue band

- on -

a white band

- on -

a field of red

1883

From the 17th to the 19th century, the flag of Thailand was plain red. When it became necessary to have a more easily identifiable flag, a white elephant, symbolising good fortune, was placed in the middle of the red field.

Red represents the blood spilled in the name of independence.

White is for purity and Buddhism.

Blue is the colour of the Thai monarchy.

1917

In the early 20th century, Thailand developed close relations to the West. The king altered the flag to a more 'modern' design. The choice of red, white and blue reflects Thailand's solidarity with its new allies; the USA, Britain and France.

THE FLAG OF
RUSSIA

A
horizontal
triband
of

 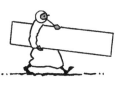  

- and -

white   blue   red

1697

Tsar Peter the Great introduced the Russian triband, inspired by the flag of the Netherlands.

1917

The Marxist Bolsheviks toppled the Tsardom and the era of Soviet Russia began. Inspired by the red flags of the French Revolution, the Soviets adopted a red banner to represent popular uprising. The hammer and sickle stood for workers and peasants. The star represented the Communist Party.

SOVIET UNION (1922–91)

Over the course of its existence, Soviet Russia expanded its territory and created the Soviet Union (USSR). In addition, it presided over the 'Eastern Bloc', a collection of Eastern European communist nations allied to the USSR. The flags of some of these states demonstrate the power of the Soviets at the time.

HUNGARIAN PEOPLE'S REPUBLIC (1949-57)

The communist star appeared on the flags of these Eastern Bloc states.

PEOPLE'S SOCIALIST REPUBLIC OF ALBANIA (1946-92)

PEOPLE'S REPUBLIC OF BULGARIA (1946-90)

SOCIALIST REPUBLIC OF ROMANIA (1947-89)

SOCIALIST FEDERAL REPUBLIC OF YUGOSLAVIA (1945-92)

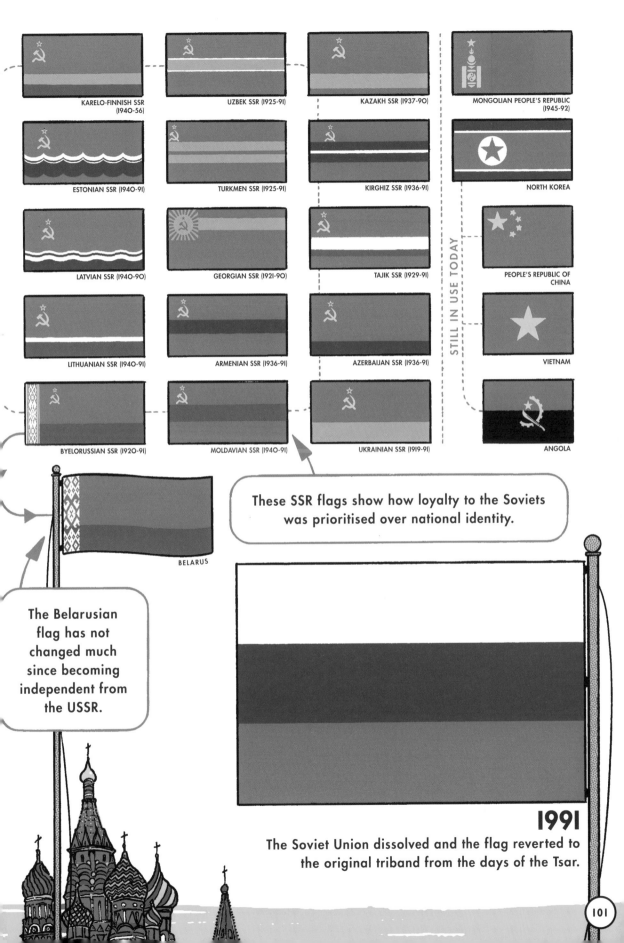

KARELO-FINNISH SSR (1940-56)

UZBEK SSR (1925-91)

KAZAKH SSR (1937-90)

MONGOLIAN PEOPLE'S REPUBLIC (1945-92)

ESTONIAN SSR (1940-91)

TURKMEN SSR (1925-91)

KIRGHIZ SSR (1936-91)

NORTH KOREA

LATVIAN SSR (1940-90)

GEORGIAN SSR (1921-90)

TAJIK SSR (1929-91)

PEOPLE'S REPUBLIC OF CHINA

LITHUANIAN SSR (1940-91)

ARMENIAN SSR (1936-91)

AZERBAIJAN SSR (1936-91)

VIETNAM

STILL IN USE TODAY

BYELORUSSIAN SSR (1920-91)

MOLDAVIAN SSR (1940-91)

UKRAINIAN SSR (1919-91)

ANGOLA

These SSR flags show how loyalty to the Soviets was prioritised over national identity.

BELARUS

The Belarusian flag has not changed much since becoming independent from the USSR.

1991

The Soviet Union dissolved and the flag reverted to the original triband from the days of the Tsar.

THE FLAG OF NEPAL

A white moon and sun - on - a red five-sided field fimbriated in blue

The war banners of ruling families in South Asia were often bordered triangular pennants. They were brightly coloured, often depicting religious symbols or symbols of allegiance.

1800s

During the rule of the Rana family (1846–1951) the two pennants were combined to form the double-triangle shape we know today. The moon and sun symbols had faces drawn on.

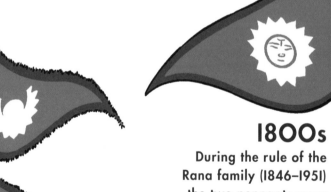

1700s

When Nepal was unified by King Prithvi Narayan Shah, he displayed two red pennants on top of one another. The sun and moon symbols related to the ruling family.

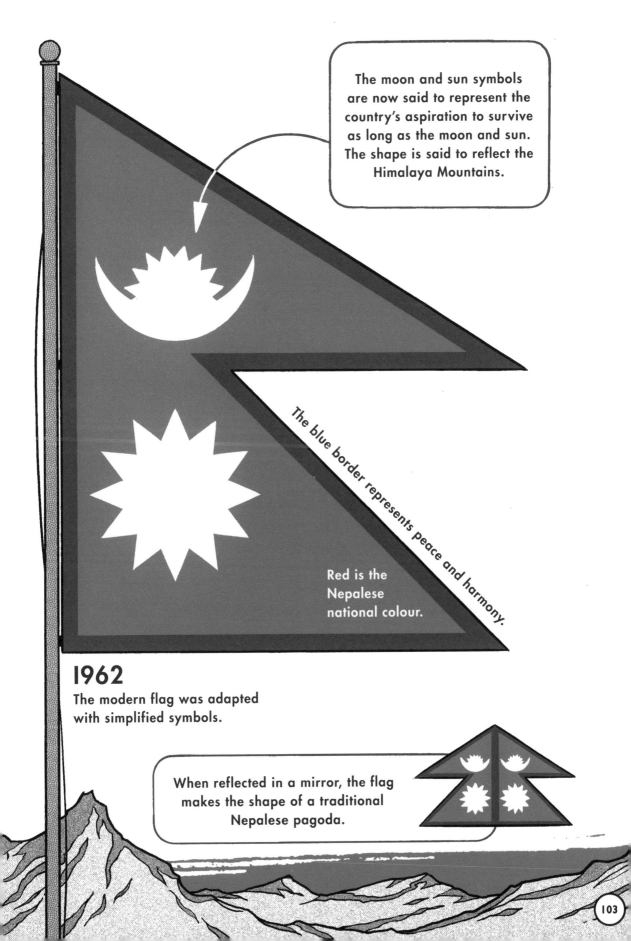

The moon and sun symbols are now said to represent the country's aspiration to survive as long as the moon and sun. The shape is said to reflect the Himalaya Mountains.

The blue border represents peace and harmony.

Red is the Nepalese national colour.

1962
The modern flag was adapted with simplified symbols.

When reflected in a mirror, the flag makes the shape of a traditional Nepalese pagoda.

THE AMERICAS

ARCTIC
OCEAN

GREENLAND
(Denmark)

USA

CANADA

UNITED STATES
OF AMERICA

ATLANTIC
OCEAN

MEXICO

GUYANA
SURINAME
FRENCH GUIANA (France)

VENEZUELA

COLOMBIA

ECUADOR

PERU

BRAZIL

PACIFIC
OCEAN

BOLIVIA

PARAGUAY

ARGEN-
TINA

URU-
GUAY

CHILE

CENTRAL AMERICA

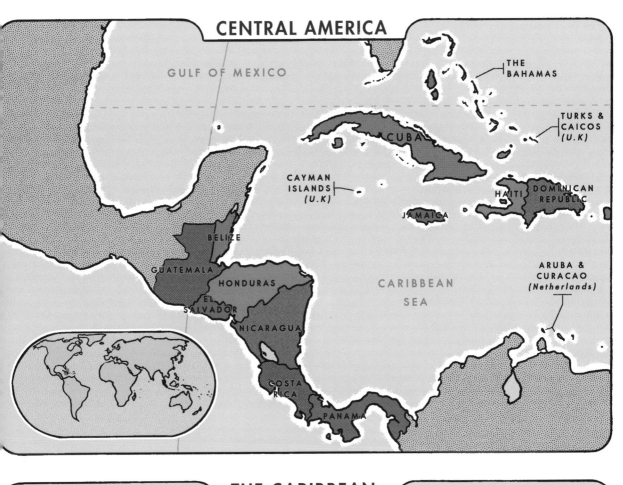

GULF OF MEXICO

THE BAHAMAS

TURKS & CAICOS (U.K)

CUBA

CAYMAN ISLANDS (U.K)

DOMINICAN REPUBLIC

HAITI

JAMAICA

BELIZE

GUATEMALA

HONDURAS

EL SALVADOR

CARIBBEAN SEA

ARUBA & CURACAO (Netherlands)

NICARAGUA

COSTA RICA

PANAMA

THE CARIBBEAN

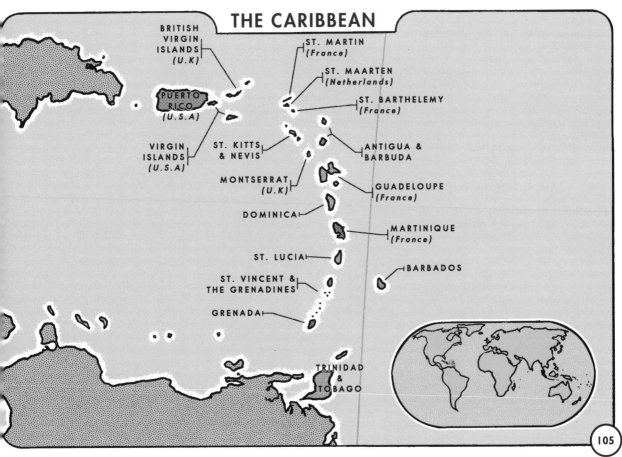

BRITISH VIRGIN ISLANDS (U.K)

ST. MARTIN (France)

ST. MAARTEN (Netherlands)

PUERTO RICO (U.S.A)

ST. BARTHELEMY (France)

VIRGIN ISLANDS (U.S.A)

ST. KITTS & NEVIS

ANTIGUA & BARBUDA

MONTSERRAT (U.K)

GUADELOUPE (France)

DOMINICA

MARTINIQUE (France)

ST. LUCIA

BARBADOS

ST. VINCENT & THE GRENADINES

GRENADA

TRINIDAD & TOBAGO

EUROPE

ICELAND

NORWAY

SWEDEN

FINLAND

ESTONIA

LATVIA

DENMARK

LITHUANIA

IRELAND

UNITED KINGDOM

NETHER-LANDS

GERMANY

POLAND

BELARUS

BELGIUM

CZECH-REPUBLIC

UKRAINE

LUXEMBOURG

ATLANTIC OCEAN

FRANCE

MOLDOVA

ROMANIA

ANDORRA

BULGARIA

PORT-UGAL

SPAIN

GREECE

GIBRALTAR (U.K)

CUETA (Spain)

MALTA

CYPRUS

SOUTH-EASTERN EUROPE

SLOVAKIA

LIECHTENSTEIN

AUSTRIA

HUNGARY

SWITZERLAND

SLOVENIA

CROATIA

ITALY

BOSNIA HERZE-GOVINA

SERBIA

SAN MARINO

MONACO

MONTE-NEGRO

KOSOVO

CORSICA (France)

VATICAN CITY

MACEDONIA

ALBANIA

SARDINIA (Italy)

AFRICA & THE MIDDLE EAST

MADEIRA
ISLANDS
(Portugal)

CANARY
ISLANDS
(Spain)

GEORGIA

AZERBAIJAN

TURKEY

ARMENIA

TUNISIA

LEBANON
ISRAEL
PALESTINE

SYRIA

IRAQ

IRAN

MOROCCO

JORDAN

KUWAIT

ALGERIA

LIBYA

EGYPT

BAHRAIN

QATAR

U.A.E

*Western
Sahara*

SAUDI
ARABIA

OMAN

MAURITANIA

MALI

NIGER

CHAD

SUDAN

ERITREA

YEMEN

SENEGAL

THE
GAMBIA

BURKINA
FASO

NIGERIA

DJIBOUTI

SOMALIA

GUINEA

GHANA

BENIN

CENTRAL
AFRICAN
REPUBLIC

SOUTH
SUDAN

ETHIOPIA

GUINEA
BISSAU

COTE
D'IVOIRE

LIBERIA

SIERRA
LEONE

TOGO

CAMEROON

EQUATORIAL
GUINEA

ATLANTIC
OCEAN

SAO TOME
& PRINCIPE

GABON

REP.
OF
THE
CONGO

RWANDA

UGANDA

KENYA

DEMOCRATIC
REPUBLIC
OF THE
CONGO

BURUNDI

SEYCHELLES

TANZANIA

COMOROS

ASCENSION
(U.K)

ANGOLA

ZAMBIA

MALAWI

MAURITIUS

MOZAMBIQUE

MADAGASCAR

ST. HELENA
(U.K)

NAMIBIA

ZIMBABWE

BOTSWANA

INDIAN
OCEAN

SWAZILAND

SOUTH
AFRICA

LESOTHO

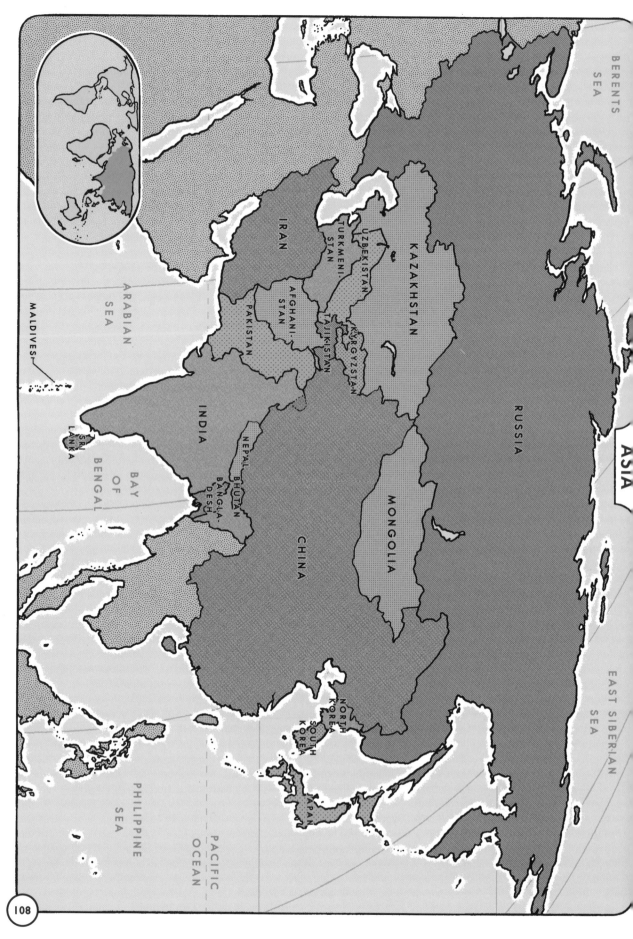

BERENTS
SEA

IRAN

TURKMENI-
STAN

UZBEKISTAN

KAZAKHSTAN

RUSSIA

ARABIAN
SEA

MALDIVES

AFGHANI-
STAN

PAKISTAN

TAJIKISTAN

KYRGYZSTAN

INDIA

SRI
LANKA

NEPAL

BHUTAN

BANGLA-
DESH

BAY
OF
BENGAL

CHINA

MONGOLIA

NORTH
KOREA

SOUTH
KOREA

JAPAN

EAST SIBERIAN
SEA

PHILIPPINE
SEA

PACIFIC
OCEAN

SOUTH-EAST ASIA

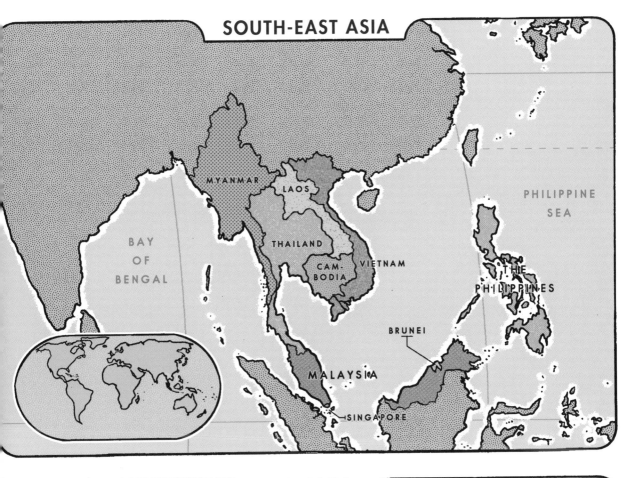

MYANMAR

LAOS

THAILAND

CAM-
BODIA

VIETNAM

BAY
OF
BENGAL

PHILIPPINE
SEA

THE
PHILIPPINES

BRUNEI

MALAYSIA

SINGAPORE

OCEANIA

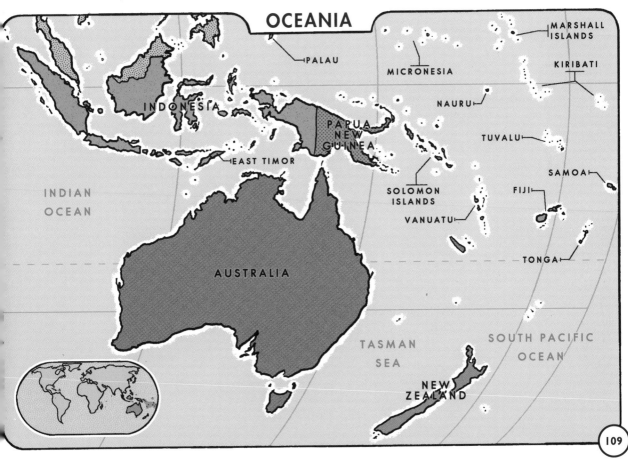

PALAU

MICRONESIA

MARSHALL
ISLANDS

KIRIBATI

NAURU

TUVALU

INDONESIA

PAPUA
NEW
GUINEA

EAST TIMOR

SOLOMON
ISLANDS

VANUATU

FIJI

SAMOA

INDIAN
OCEAN

TONGA

AUSTRALIA

TASMAN
SEA

SOUTH PACIFIC
OCEAN

NEW
ZEALAND

FLYING COLOURS
Published by Cicada Books Limited

Written, illustrated and designed by Robert G Fresson
Additional text by Robin Jacobs

British Library Cataloguing-in-Publication Data.

A CIP record for this book is available from the British Library.
ISBN: 978-1-908714-46-6

Cicada Books Limited
48 Burghley Road
London
NW5 1UE

E: cicadabooks@gmail.com
W: www.cicadabooks.co.uk

Printed in China

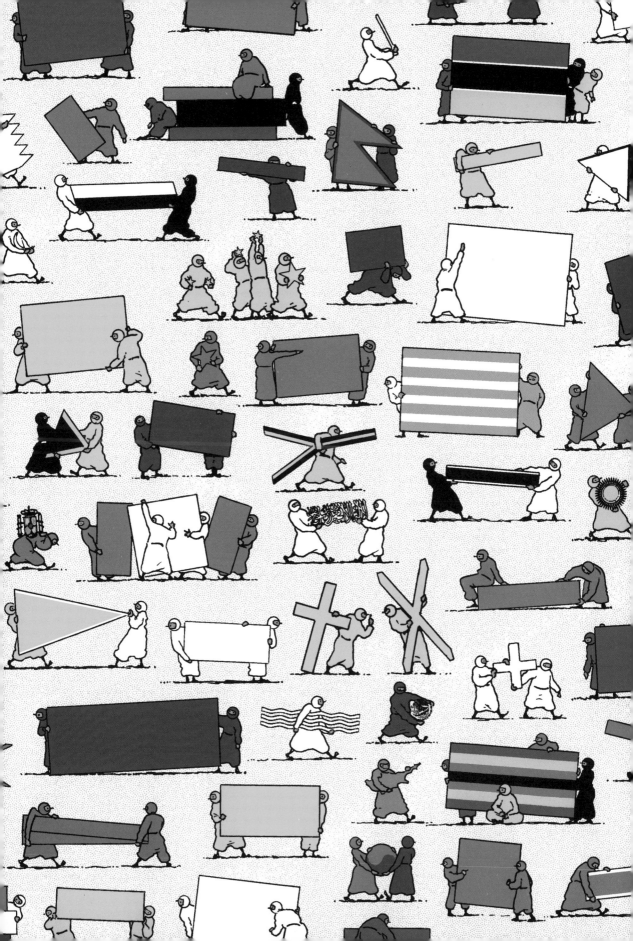